FINDING TRUE BALANCE

Great Balancing Acts of Life

FINDING TRUE BALANCE

Great Balancing Acts of Life

James LeVoy Sorenson

BOOKCRAFT
SALT LAKE CITY, UTAH

Library of Congress Cataloging-in-Publication Data

Sorenson, James LeVoy.
    Finding true balance / James LeVoy Sorenson.
        p.   cm.
Includes index.
    ISBN 1-57008-778-4 (pbk.)
    1. Christian life—Mormon authors. I. Title.

BX8656 .S67 2001
248.4'89332—dc21   2001004998

Printed in the United States of America   72082-6908
Publishers Press, Salt Lake City, UT

10   9   8   7   6   5   4   3   2   1

MY INFLUENCE

My life shall touch many lives
Before this day is done
Leave marks of good or ill,
Before the setting evening sun.
The prayer this day I pray,
My life helps other lives
That have passed this way.

Life is a constant stream of footprints,
Fingerprints, and thoughts.
None to be replicated,
None disappear without a trace.

Let not this day go by
At home, at work, or play
Until someone is happier
Because I passed this way.

ACKNOWLEDGMENTS

∽o∽

I would like to credit past teachers and mentors who have influenced my thinking. They have ignited my imagination and inspired my innovations. I invite everyone who reads this to take ownership as I have taken ownership from others.

To all those above and below, I convey my gratitude, thanks, and love.

I want to thank Daniel P. Sorensen for his editing, unique talent, and expertise. I also want to thank Gloria Smith for her ongoing loyalty, dedication, and hard work.

CONTENTS

∽◦∾

II. MOTION

III. RHYTHM

TABLE OF FIGURES

∽○∾

PREFACE

∾◦∾

Balance is the secret of life. All our dimensions must be in balance for us to be happy. We must find balance in our personal lives and in our social interactions. Personal balance occurs when our physical, intellectual, and spiritual dimensions are in harmony. Social balance results from a delicate interplay of family, neighborhood, and community.

But what exactly is balance? And why do we find it hard to achieve balance in our lives? I believe it's because we have a mistaken idea of what balance is. Balance is not something we attain, a plateau we reach, a destination we arrive at. Attaining True Balance is a continuing process. Ever changing and evolving, the quest for balance is a dynamic process of learning, becoming, and giving. True Balance begins with God and is ever and always informed by love.

Our happiness, success, and survival depend, I believe, upon the extent to which we participate in God's finely tuned and delicately calibrated balance, which is manifest in all of nature. But obtaining nature's balance, or True Balance, is more than arriving at a state of simple equilibrium. It is an active, vibrant, dynamic process, a continuum that is always in motion. We exist three-dimensionally in a basic creation of solids, liquids, and gases, modulated in time, energy, and motion, and measured by past, present, and future.

The three basic elements of True Balance are dimension, motion, and rhythm.

Dimension describes our position in a world measured by height, width, and depth. The three dimensions of our world have profound implications for how we perceive, think, and act. I will develop these implications throughout the course of the book. For now, I want you to keep in mind how important the "third dimension" is in all aspects of life. For me, looking for the third dimension means going beyond conventional wisdom; it means looking for the bigger picture. Most important, looking for the third dimension means searching for knowledge and "finding the better way."

The second element of True Balance is motion. Everything in life is in continual motion, powered by dynamic energy. Electrons spin around the nucleus of an atom, planets swing around the sun, galaxies swirl through the universe. Only by actively and energetically moving forward can we learn to emulate God, our Creator, and profit from nature's dynamic motion. Putting the moving world to work for us is finding the better way.

The third element of True Balance is rhythm. Rhythm is measured by time and defined by change. Night follows day, the ocean ebbs and flows, seasons change. We breathe in and we breathe out. Our hearts contract and expand. Life is always in motion but not always at the same pace. The rhythms of nature teach us to find our own rhythm and pace ourselves to "find the better way."

Dimension, motion, rhythm. These are the constituents of True Balance. The three together make up True Balance, but each alone is an exemplar of True Balance. Dimension is balance in space, motion is balance in energy, and rhythm is balance in time.

The most precise formulation of True Balance would be three-dimensional, rhythmic motion. I like to use the following formula to define my theory of True Balance: $E = MB^3/R$, which is Excellence equals Motion Balanced in three dimensions, modulated by Rhythm.

INTRODUCTION: THE BALANCE OF LIFE

ᙄᴗᙆ

Wings of the Butterfly

God has created the progressive and presiding principle of balance in all parts of nature. Whether it be atoms or galaxies, everything moves in a delicate and calibrated rhythm. This exquisite balance of life is manifest in every link of the great chain of being; it modulates the entire dimension of the universe. To me it is both astonishing and profound that in physical size, human beings are midway between the universe itself and the smallest, subatomic particle—astonishing because we tend to be conscious only of the sheer size of the physical world while ignoring the microscopic gradations of subatomic matter. Profound because it demonstrates that humankind is at the very fulcrum of organized creation and the measure of all things.

Nature is a system, and everything in a system affects everything else. The beating of a butterfly's wings creates an infinitesimal change in the atmosphere, but the movement becomes part of the force that initiates a monsoon on the other side of the globe. A family is a system. What happens to one family member affects all of the others. We commiserate in each other's troubles and participate in each other's happiness.

Ultimately, we are all brothers and sisters. The world is our family. Our hearts beat as one.

We are an inextricable part of the system that is the world, and each of us plays a necessary part in balancing the whole. I sit on a chair in my office, and that chair rests on the floor of my building on West Temple Street in South Salt Lake. The building itself rests on the valley floor that is part of the earth's crust.

Whatever I do, therefore, I participate in the balanced rhythm and motion of the world. My body and the "body" of the earth move in harmony. In fact, according to the principles of physics, the earth rises ever so infinitesimally to accept my step; gravity is the third dimension that marries body and earth. The balance essential in walking can only be understood as a relationship of my body to the ground on which it rests and moves, stands and walks. The earth is there to meet each foot as it falls, and I walk with the faith that the ground will support me.

The Economy of Nature

God's creations, from cell to solar system to galaxy, are continually in the process of creating and recreating themselves. Atom balances atom as cell balances cell in a process of constant recalibration. Your heart beats in a precise rhythm, systole answering diastole. Every plant is a balanced system, roots reaching downward to gather nutrients for the limbs, which stretch upward to absorb energy from the sun.

The economy of nature is displayed in the fine balance between men and

Figure 1– The Atom

women. Estrogen in women and testosterone in men not only determine physical development but also define gender in an incalculable number of ways—everything from psychological disposition to physiological response. Nevertheless, each gender carries in its blood the hormones of the other. Men and women are balanced not only by differences but also by similarities. The so-called war between the sexes is in reality an intricate dance, a very delicate balancing act. Men and women are defined by their relationships to one another; they are made to fit and flower together, not to bloom and die alone.

Look at the larger sphere of life outside and around us. We are immersed in multitudes of intricate balancing acts. Have you ever contemplated the system of an ant colony or the formation of birds in flight or the buzzing cooperation of a beehive? What appears to be competition among species is, on a larger view, filled with reciprocity and cooperation. Organisms in the ecosystem adapt to and support each other. Trees lift their limbs one upon another with such symmetry, pattern, and balance that the forest survives and thrives as a single organism.

Even the waste products of one species are vital to another's survival; one species' resources are replenished by another's. Photosynthesis is an elegant example of nature's balance. Green plants reduce harmful levels of carbon dioxide by synthesizing it with water and sunlight to supply animal life with oxygen. Thus something potentially lethal to humans—carbon dioxide—is transformed into something vital to sustain and fuel our lives—oxygen. All ecologies that we understand operate on the principle of win-win. In its perfect economy, nature seeks a balance. In God's creations, nothing disappears without a trace—nothing is ever completely wasted or lost.

This economy of nature is at work even in the destructive forces of tornadoes, earthquakes, landslides, blizzards, fire, drought, and floods. From such destruction comes renewal and

Figure 2– Earth As Seen from Miles Out in Space

new life. The tide goes all the way out and comes all the way in. Day balances night. Summer balances winter. All things return to dust as part of God's balanced economy. Nature is ever in renewal, and in its rhythmic cycle, life balances death.

A conversation about life and death has stayed with me for forty years. In 1959, while attending a meeting at the King's Hotel in St. Louis, I was talking with a rabbi about the nature of life. This is what he told me: "We enter this world with our fists tightly clenched and our mouths open, gasping for air. Then all of us depart this world in exactly the opposite state— our hands open, with palms upward, as our last breath leaves our open lips. We take nothing with us." Every physical thing we've gotten, we give back.

At first, I thought what the rabbi had said was contrary to what I believed. Now I realize he was stating a fundamental, eternal truth. At the end of our mortal life we are perfectly balanced, at rest and at peace. Whatever we've acquired in life, we give back in our physical death. This giving exemplifies the basic rule of life: giving always completes the cycle of becoming, achieving, and getting.

You Are Unique

A free falling drop of water forms a beautiful, three-dimensionally balanced sphere, but at a given velocity and temperature, it changes into a snowflake, also balanced and beautifully symmetrical. Each snowflake is a unique and individual creation, never to be replicated. Each of us is similarly individual and unique. Though mortality may seem as transitory as melting snowflakes, each of us leaves an individual mark as distinct and unique as our DNA and our fingerprints. Our individual presence is a present to the world.

Our DNA expresses our uniqueness, but it also connects us to innumerable generations before us. DNA, with its sequence of symbolic letters, can be seen as God's own algebra, a never-ending equation of life. Each of us plays a unique part in that equation. The human genome has now been mapped, and the code of life will not only extend the reach of our genealogy but also unite generation to generation, the hearts of the children turned toward the fathers and the hearts of the fathers turned toward the children.

People naturally look for similarities between children and parents. My wife, Beverley, was introducing our youngest daughters, Gail and Chris, to an acquaintance, who immediately said, "Well, I can see that Gail is your daughter, but Chris doesn't look like you at all!" Admittedly, Chris was not immediately recognizable as Beverley's daughter. When she was a baby people affectionately called her "little Jamie" because they thought she looked so much like her daddy.

I see a different mixture of traits in each of our children and grandchildren. For example, I look at my grandsons Robert and

David (who are brothers) and see how different each of them is in size, inclination, and personality.

Despite the obvious differences, as each generation yields to the next, similarities, resemblance, and continuities endure. Robert looks more like me and seems to have inherited some of the same entrepreneurial instincts. When he was fourteen, he came to me with an idea to start a business using junked mail trucks—he wanted to fix them up with bells and whistles and go around neighborhoods selling popcorn. "You get a better margin selling popcorn than you do by just selling candy or ice cream," he confided to me.

Robert's cousin Brian offers another contrast. He's right on task, saving up money for his Mormon mission, while Robert—true to his original style—worries his mom by such adventures as climbing the old smelter smokestack in Murray, Utah. Brian is great with computers: with his digital wizardry, a job that would normally take twenty hours a week to complete took him just a few minutes a day.

I could give similar examples about each of my children and grandchildren and tell stories about how they always surprise me when I think I've got them categorized, graded, and completely figured out. The uniqueness of each member of a family is an evidence of the balance inherent in every system in God's creation. Such uniqueness encourages competition and co-operation, both of which are necessary for us not just to survive but to grow and prosper.

The chaotic, ever-changing imbalance of modern life can, however, put the uniqueness of our children at peril. On my office desk I have matching photographs of myself in 1923 as a two-year-old in Rexburg, Idaho, and my two-year-old grandson Jacob Harris in April of 1999. In those photos I see what we've lost in our accelerated modern age. There I am, a smiling and secure tot from a vanished era, comfortable in the cycle of seasons and the rhythm of planting and harvesting. But in Jacob's face I see the insecurity that is the product of our stressed-out, over-indulged, and fast-paced age. His smile is not as carefree and relaxed as mine at the same age, 76 years ago.

Figure 3– James L. Sorenson and Jacob Harris

Rexburg, Idaho 1923   Salt Lake City, Utah 1999

I'd like to see relaxed and confident smiles on all my grand-children's faces and give them the keys to a more balanced, joy-ful, and uncomplicated life.

As I see the wonder, glory, and uniqueness in my children, grandchildren, and great-grandchildren, I want to expand the potential of all children so they can find and develop their unique talents. At the Sorenson Multicultural Center in Salt Lake City, deprived children have a chance to play basketball, swim, dance, and box. The kids at the center log on to the computers for hours—sometimes absorbed in their exploration of cyberspace until midnight—reluctant to return to empty houses and dysfunctional families. Playing sports and mastering computers renews their spirits and builds self-confidence and promotes self-esteem, providing a sense of real accomplishment in their otherwise sterile lives. As a larger world opens up to them, they expand their horizons and learn about life beyond their limited environments and rundown neighborhoods.

The year the center opened, the decline in gang activity in the city was less than one percent, but in the next year, as activity at the center expanded, gang activity decreased forty-five percent. In recent years, we've been able to help reduce gang activities in central Salt Lake City by seventy-three percent.

Kids join gangs because they are lonely. The gang gives them a ready-made identity. Those who join don't realize that the gang ultimately manipulates them and makes them hostage to the larger group. Gangs lack balance because everything is geared to an aggressive, one-dimensional group identity. Gang membership robs kids of all their God-given individuality, identity, and uniqueness and stifles their development.

Figure 4– James Luke, James Lee, James LeVoy Sorenson
White Sage Ranch 1999

Becoming Our Best

God pulls grass, flowers, and trees upward against the force of gravity. In order to prosper, all living things must move against the force of gravity three-dimensionally, while balancing in motion. The harmony, order, and three-dimensional balance in nature—every element measured by the force of gravity—inspire me to know God and try to imitate his beautiful plan in my life. God's laws govern the larger universe, and they govern our individual lives.

Just as the sun causes the flowers to bloom and the trees to reach skyward, God, our Creator, pulls us upward out of ourselves and beckons us to be more than creatures that merely eat and sleep. It is my belief that we are here on earth to create and become more human through choice and the use of moral agency. Human beings trying to be spiritual are really spiritual beings trying to be human.

We are at our best and most creative when we strive to imitate our Creator in our own sphere. We must seek balance in ourselves and in our relationships. We must constantly mix, blend, and nurture to keep the right balance, whatever the issue, whatever the problem, whatever the goal. As God's children and inhabitants of the earth, we are stewards of what he has created.

This is a philosophy of life based on natural law; it reflects what our limited human intelligence can discern about the mind of God. Natural law is not just a true description of how the world works, it is truth and beauty in action and surely reveals God's love for the created world. Truth is the most beautiful thing there is, and we intuitively seek it everywhere, whatever our desire, whatever our inclination, whatever our interest. As we find a balance in all aspects of nature, we ought to always examine the concept of balance in our personal lives. We find the full meaning of faith, hope, and love in achieving true balance in life.

We succeed and progress in our endeavors only to the degree that we keep our lives in proper balance. True Balance is never stationary; it is dynamic and ever in motion, ever in the process of becoming. A conversation between O Sensei, the founder of aikido, and a student, illustrates the concept of True Balance.

After a match, the master was praised by the student for never falling.

"You have perfect balance," said the student.

"You are wrong," said Sensei. "My skill is not perfect balance. When I start to fall, I have the ability to regain my balance."

Ever in motion, True Balance keeps you from falling.

The more precisely balanced we become, the more we achieve. We become healthier, happier, wiser.

The Gift of Learning

Learning is at the heart of becoming our best. Learning is as vital an exercise to the brain as aerobic exercise is to the body. If you think of your brain as "hardware," then your mind, spirit, and senses are the "software." The types of software—our thoughts, habits, and desires—determine how much brain power we are able to develop and utilize.

Many people confine their brains to just one kind of interest, a single dogma, or one type of software. That is like trying to make the whole of all your experiences fit into a single spreadsheet. The more things you know, the larger your vision of life. The more varied your experience, the better equipped you are to master new experience and prosper in new circumstances. The more you know, the better your balance. You can adjust your gait to new terrain.

Learning is a process that is itself part of a tripartite structure. I see it this way:

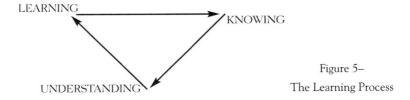

LEARNING → KNOWING

UNDERSTANDING

Figure 5—
The Learning Process

Learning is where the triangle begins. Our senses are the portals through which we get in touch with the outside world, and they serve as doors of perception and knowledge. It is by seeing, hearing, touching, tasting, and smelling that learning takes place.

Knowing, the second side of the triangle, is more cerebral. After we learn things about the world through our senses, our minds sort the data into categories. It might seem that knowing is more a state than a process. When we say we know something, we might feel we are merely describing something that has already taken place. It feels as though we "own" something, such as a car, a house, or a pair of shoes.

But knowing, like everything else, is a matter of motion. Knowing is an active process, an active exercise of mind over the particulars of our learned experience. It's dangerous to think you know it all because then you think you don't have anything else to learn. That's why I often greet people around the office by asking, "What have you learned today?"

Understanding is the third side of the triangle. Again, at first it may seem that understanding is a static principle. Even the root words, *standing under*, suggest something unmoving; but like learning and knowing, understanding is a condition of the mind that is always in motion. Let's keep the image of "standing under" but add one of my favorite axioms—put your bushel basket under a tree where the fruit will fall. You can't just stand in one place; you must keep your eyes open and your feet moving to reap the best fruits of life.

Learn All Your Life

Too many people associate learning only with formal schooling—memorizing the multiplication tables or reciting world capitals. Once out of school, their learning clocks stop. Before the advent of quartz watches, we had "self-winding" watches, which meant that the mainspring was kept at the proper tension by the motion of your arm. Those who stop learning after they leave school are like people with self-winding watches who stop moving their arms. To further demonstrate this analogy: the balance wheel inside the watch needs the tension or energy of motion to keep the watch ticking. When people stop learning, their internal balance wheels lose positive tension and energy. Their mental clocks stop.

True learning is like True Balance: it has its own motion and rhythm. True learning is not just pumping information into your brain. It is an art form. It means paying attention to your environment, sorting sensory experience into categories, and bringing synergy to your experience so you can confidently and boldly act on it. True learning requires the ability to conceptualize, remember, and recall. True learning is listening to your own mind, making choices, and formulating a strategy of how to act and react in the world.

There is also a geometry to true learning. Geometry literally means "measuring the earth," and learning requires us to take the measure of our environment and our place in it. The mathematics of geometry involve axioms about the relationships between points, lines, planes, figures, surfaces, and solids; solid geometry in particular is a method for taking the measure of our three-dimensional world. To me, geometry provides a metaphor for how we should encounter our external world, always looking for axioms that help us in our quest for understanding. The geometry of learning is not just mathematics, but a way of life.

At the heart of true, lifelong learning are the arts—music, dance, painting, theater, sculpture, literature, and poetry. Nothing is more satisfying to the soul. Inherent in the arts are the qualities of True Balance: motion, rhythm, and dimension. The arts stimulate us through their various rhythms, helping us to expand our perception and sharpen our appreciation of the larger dimensions of life. To me it's obvious that the arts should be at the center of formal education. But unfortunately the arts often get pushed to the periphery. Great emphasis is put on technical training, but such training in the absence of liberal arts detaches the student from an essential element of life, leaving him imprisoned in the two-dimensional process of stimulus and response.

So we need to teach music and art and poetry in our schools. By the time we leave formal education, we should have a strong base from which to appreciate and participate in the arts on our own. Possessing that, we will have the skills to continually educate ourselves, to refine and calibrate the True Balance that empowers us to learn, grow, and prosper. For me, poetry and music, coming together to create song, have been both a rich source and a profound expression of True Balance. Writing poems and songs has put me in touch with a dimension bigger than myself. Conceiving the words and music have transported me to new realms of truth and beauty.

It's been said that when we're through learning, we're through living. Most of my personal and business success has come from looking farther ahead, learning faster, and burning brighter and longer than others might. I'm a great believer in formal education, but the false pride that sometimes comes with academic honors can blind us. "Being taught" doesn't necessarily mean you've learned anything. In fact, you can become so fixated on facts and information that you lose the curiosity and creativity that true education ought to foster. I succeeded as a pharmaceutical salesman because I was not locked into the rigid categories of a formal education. I compensated for my lack of a pharmaceutical degree by eagerly learning everything I could about new trends and state-of-the-art pharmaceuticals.

I remember when a new drug called cyclogesterin first came on the market. It was designed to help women become pregnant, and I felt that the drug would be of great benefit. After studying and memorizing all the technical literature and learning that the drug had the power to balance hormones, I felt confident touting the drug to physicians. Cyclogesterin helped a great number of childless people become parents.

My lack of a formal degree didn't hinder my success during the uranium boom, either. I knew that I had a lot to learn, so I did my homework daily and didn't just speculate on the basis of imagined competence or quick riches.

I also did my homework as I formed other companies. I had a yearning to constantly gain new knowledge. When you develop this "out of school" attitude about learning, it grows stronger and stays with you longer.

People ask me why I'm always delving into so many leading-edge technologies, such as those being developed at Sorenson Vision or the innovative DNA genetic sequencing methods at Sorenson BioScience. The answer is simple: I'm curious about life and eager to learn more. In this moving world, I've always enjoyed the challenge of moving with it and learning from it. I enjoy being on the leading edge, staying in a learning mode, always looking for the better way. I like the challenge of look-ing for new ways to improve, extend, and save lives. The things I can do to help others bring me my greatest satisfactions and rewards.

When people look at me they wonder what makes me tick, where I'm hiding it, and when it's going to stop ticking. But after eight decades of life, I feel as though I'm just beginning. I don't want to close the book—I want to keep turning those pages! I want to write new chapters, word by word, line by line, day by day. As time keeps ticking, the more I learn, and the more I want to learn. My curiosity increases every day. Each day comes bearing its new gifts. All we have to do is untie the ribbons.

Keep learning, or your mind will become stiff, brittle, and slack, just as your bones and muscles will if you don't exercise them. Your mind wants to move no matter what, and the grooves it moves in just keep getting deeper. It's like playing the same song on an old 33-rpm record. It goes around and around, and pretty soon all you hear is scratching and static. The grooves get so deep that your mind gets stuck. If you keep learning, creating new grooves in your brain, you continue remaking, refining, and defining yourself—yesterday an LP, today an 8-track tape, tomorrow a CD. Keep learning and your awareness of the world will become richer, deeper, and more profound. The more you learn, the more the world reveals itself as a palace filled with wonder.

The more you learn, the more you're able to learn. As my mother used to say, "Be careful what you put into your brain. Whatever you are today, you become more so . . . day by day." If you elevate your thoughts, you will strengthen your attention, deepen your intuition, and expand your vision in your quest to attain your highest goals and reach your fullest potential.

A passion for learning acknowledges and celebrates the generations that have come and gone before us. We walk in their footsteps and see farther by climbing the monuments others have built.

Generations

I didn't realize it at the time, but my first lesson in the importance of balance came from my dad. "Pace yourself," he would say. "Seek to understand and strive to stay within your own rhythm." When I look back on how he went about his work and how he lived his life, I realize that he was saying, "Find your own balance." And my mother, too, taught me lessons in balance. Her focus was on behavior, and how I needed to be careful not to go to extremes—how to find the right balance of virtues.

The lessons I learned from them have been validated by my own experiences. In all aspects of life—spiritual, intellectual, and physical—balance is the presiding concept. This matter of finding your own balance shows itself in all sorts of interesting ways. Energy is the key component of balance, and Dad's philosophy of pacing yourself is really about calibrating your energy. When I was a kid, I remember him shaking his head about all the energy I was expending playing basketball.

"All that running up and down the court is wasted energy," he would say. "You'd be better off putting all that energy to doing some productive work, like digging trenches." But the energy I put into basketball paid off in a big way when I won a college scholarship. The physical energy I put into basketball, which seemed to Dad a lot of foolishness, actually gave me the chance to expand my intellectual dimension. I paced myself differently than Dad. I found my own balance.

Today, a critical element in maintaining my personal balance is playing squash. It's an activity that fits in well with how I pace my day. I have found that being on the court for an hour, exercising my body, stimulates intellectual energy for all my projects. An energy exchange takes place that fosters True Balance.

My oldest son, Jim, finds his balance by playing golf, which seems to me to take up a lot of time. When I hear myself telling Jim that golf is a waste of time, I realize I sound just like Dad telling me basketball is a waste of energy. I have to remind myself that each person has to find his own balance. And just as basketball led to my success in another sphere, so golf has paid off for Jim in his business. Golf gives you a chance to size up the other guy, and the rhythm of the game allows for quite a bit of leisurely business discussion.

Golf fits Jim's temperament and restores his balance in the same way that squash fits my temperament and restores my balance. I keep coming back to my dad's admonition: "Find *your own* rhythm and pace yourself."

Here's another example of why you need to find your own rhythm and pace yourself to achieve True Balance. I like to "go for a walk" on my treadmill to get myself going in the morning. The electronic display lets me know the incline, how fast I'm going, how long I've been walking, and how far I've gone. The distance "traveled" is of course a product of speed and time. To go the distance and get the maximum benefit from the treadmill, I have to pace myself and find the rhythm that best balances time and speed.

To stay in control and keep my balance on the machine, I must adjust my stride to the angle of the incline. To stay perpendicular and upright, I must lean into the slope. The steeper I set the incline, the longer my stride must be to stay in balance. My stride is different than yours, and the angle of the incline will vary according to age, inclination, and circumstances. Find the balance that best suits you.

I recommend you challenge yourself with increasingly steeper inclines. A steeper incline gives you a stronger heart. A steeper incline calls forth your best effort.

When the ground is level, when there are few challenges, you can become apathetic and bored, constantly in danger of losing your balance. You can easily nod off and sleepwalk through life. The seeming ease of going downhill can be deceptive, but even there you must hold yourself back to remain perpendicular and avoid falling forward. However, it is in struggling on the upward slopes that our best effort is required and progression toward achieving True Balance is most pronounced. Always focus on a point a good distance ahead, which in life means having a goal you're continually moving toward.

These practical lessons in "finding your own balance" have profound implications in the art of living. I repeat—in all dimensions: spiritual, intellectual, and physical—balance is always the progressive and presiding principle.

I
DIMENSION

1

THE THREE-LEGGED STOOL

You often hear people talk about balance, but it's usually a balance of this and that, X and Y, black and white, left and right. They talk about balancing career with family, freedom with responsibility, the spiritual with the physical. This is true, of course, but it's limiting because it implies only two possibilities. When you say you need a balance of X and Y, you lock yourself into looking at things in a flat, two-dimensional way. You become a prisoner of dualistic thinking: saint or sinner, mind or matter, up or down, positive or negative.

That's a two-dimensional, black or white solution. Such over-simplification leaves you holding only one end of the stick. To say that you should always be positive rather than negative is like saying that everything should always be white rather than black. Our three-dimensional life is actually much more complex. People whose attitude becomes too positive often fail. I believe in being positive, while working hard to balance it with reality. I will take risks only when I think the odds are highly in my favor. Before I rush into anything, I always look for at least three basic, favorable elements in a given situation, rather than just one or two.

The often overlooked third dimension is frequently discovered by intuition. Instinct tells us to go ahead or pull back. An example of this intuitive grasp of the third dimension occurred years ago when I was in the process of buying a flour mill. All the formalities were in place and the papers were ready to be signed. But a feeling of uncertainty and doubt persisted; something was "missing"—so I withdrew my offer. It turned out to be a wise decision. My intuition (the third dimension) had warned me that the flour mill would be a losing proposition.

Negative emotion can be a warning that a vital dimension is missing. Introspection and reflection can bring about a recalibration and rebalancing of how you use time and energy. See negative feelings as a sign that you need to reevaluate or go in a different direction. When you're out of touch or out of sorts, you're out of balance. Think of it as a car with its wheels out of alignment. It can reach the point where you lose control and crash.

Keeping your balance requires a sharp focus, a sure sense of where you are, and a keen awareness of the forces in play within and around you. Stop, look, and listen. Know the ground on which you stand. The importance of being "grounded" can be demonstrated by an analogy with electricity. With positive and negative charges flowing through a circuit, you need something connected to the earth, which significantly remains at a constant potential—in other words, electrically balanced.

Think of the third dimension as the electrical ground. If you get yourself caught in a two-way oscillation of positive and negative forces, you can get badly burned. Make sure that you look for the ground wire to keep three-dimensional balance and protect yourself against being burned by dangerous dualism.

Dualistic thinking engenders oscillation. You swing from one extreme to the other, never moving out of two dimensions. We live in a three-dimensional world, and for things to remain upright, they must balance in three dimensions. A simple example is the three-legged stool or tripod. A stool with only one or two legs will easily tip over. Three legs are the minimum requirement for the stool to remain balanced and stable. If we were living in a two-dimensional world, two legs would be sufficient. But our world is three-dimensional, and balance therefore always requires at least three elements. Approaching things from a single or dual perspective limits your potential and your achievement.

You might say, "That's all well and good about stools and tripods, but we're human beings, and we get along just fine with two legs. If balance in three dimensions is so important, why don't we have three legs or a tail like a kangaroo?" For one thing, we are creatures in motion and two legs are sufficient to maintain balance as we move forward, our rhythmic helical movement providing us with a triadic balance with each forward step. Compare our mode of movement with the kangaroo. That unfortunate critter has to hop—think of the energy expended—and can keep its balance only by resting on its tail, making itself into a kind of a three-legged stool.

The Smallest Necessary Number

The concept of the "fundamental three" also applies to our anatomy. Try standing on your heels. You are only able to do so if you also move this way and that. So to keep balance while standing still, we rely on the triangular form of our feet, with the heel, big, and little toes serving as corners of a modified isosceles triangle.

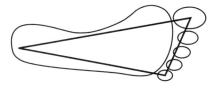

Figure 6– The Body's Balance Points
Balancing points in the body are found on the bottom of the foot.

But what about acrobats who can balance on just one hand or one finger? That seems to disprove my idea of needing two legs in motion to stay in three-dimensional balance. It appears as though the acrobats aren't moving and that everything is balanced on one tiny point. But if you look again you can see the subtle motion that enables them to maintain their balance. The other limbs may not be touching the ground, but they are postured and positioned in a three-dimensional configuration. You can balance on one foot, as long as your other leg and your arms function as counterbalances.

Not too long ago, I was fooling around in the locker room after playing squash, standing on one foot to show how well I could still keep my balance. But then I broke my own rule about balanced posture by reaching down to pick up a towel. Down I went. I ended up with some stitches in my head and a busted collarbone. I may have performed that little feat easily when I was younger, but after my miscalculation, I decided I'd better calibrate just a little more precisely the limitations imposed by age.

I guess you could say I've learned from my mistakes because I can repeat them exactly! Not long after the locker room tumble, I lost my balance while trying to get on a horse. While I had only one foot in the stirrup, the horse reared up, and I fell under him and into the dust with a thud. That really shook me up! Then a few months later, I was up at our summer place on the Weber River walking on one of three round 1000-gallon propane tanks. I thought it would be an easy jump from one tank to the other to take meter readings.

But again, the "motion" component of my balance equation wasn't equal to the task. I didn't have enough speed to complete my jump from tank to tank, and the next thing I knew, I was sprawled across one of them, flat on my back. I really banged up my left hip and had an ugly, swollen bruise all the way from my knee up to my waist and back around to my rear end. Luckily, I didn't break any bones, but I was laid up for eight weeks, which gave me some time to contemplate how foolish I had been to act like a daredevil.

That was the third time—that significant three again—in a year that I had been taught a lesson about balance. It was a sure sign to me that I should use more caution and show more respect for the wise injunction to "stop, look, and listen." But since I always look for the positive, I saw the bruises as evidence of how the body begins the process of healing and regains its systemic equilibrium so beautifully and so quickly.

The Golden Mean

Every dualistic concept has an implicit third dimension. When you couple or balance two things, you invariably come up with a third. This was the basis of Aristotle's *Ethics*, a practical and down-to-earth book on how to live. Aristotle's Golden Mean represents the balance of an intermediate state. Courage, for instance, is the intermediate state between foolhardiness and cowardice. You don't want to be afraid of everything, nor do you want to be afraid of nothing. If you're one or the other, you're a one- or two-legged stool, and chances are you'll end up flat on your face.

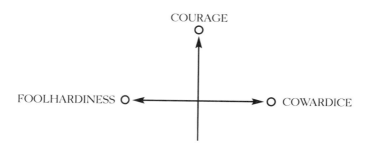

Figure 7– The Golden Mean or Middle Way

The concept of the Golden Mean is not unique to European or Western culture. In the East, Taoism teaches the Middle Way. Like the Golden Mean, the Middle Way is not a method of compromise, of splitting the difference between extremes. It envisions a third alternative for living a meaningful life.

The danger of extremes can be illustrated with a spinning top. If in its spinning, the top gets lopsided and out of balance, it will wobble, tilt, and slow to a stop. Even a balanced top will wobble if pressure is applied at the periphery. The axis must remain balanced to keep the spinning top in motion. When you abandon your center and wander toward the extreme edge, you are in danger of tilting into a fall. Going to extremes in business, politics, religion, or personal behavior requires increasing expenditures of energy to stay in balance. When everything is in balance, when the Golden Mean is being observed, less energy is needed to keep things in motion.

Another instructive way to think about the Golden Mean and moderation is to consider a concept from pharmacology. When I was working for the Upjohn Company, I was struck by the basic triadic principle of dosage, regimen, and protocol—DRP for short. Dosage is how much, regimen is when, and protocol is how. When administering drugs, if you don't carefully calibrate each procedure, you can do more harm than good. To provide benefit, dosage, regimen, and protocol must be continually monitored and delicately balanced.

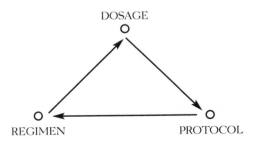

Figure 8– Dosage, Protocol, and Regimen

Drugs can carry us to a cure, a restoration of health, or to dynamic vitality. But they can also lead us down a path of abuse to destruction and death. With the proper regimen and protocol, a small dose of dextroamphetamine is a harmless central nervous system stimulant. It acts like coffee to increase alertness but doesn't have coffee's side effects, such as increased stomach acid and elevated blood pressure.

The problem in using something like dextroamphetamine is in ignoring the principle of DRP. A deadly overdose can occur if any of the three elements—dosage, regimen, or protocol—is missing. You can take too much of it (dosage). You can take it too often (regimen). And you can take it improperly, such as injecting it directly into a vein (protocol). When any of these three elements is compromised, the drug can overwhelm your system and produce harmful effects.

In illicit drug lingo, amphetamines are known as "speed," and the cautionary slogan, "Speed kills," is right on the mark. As the 16th century Swiss physician Paracelsus said, "The poison is in the dose." Just as imbalance in administering government can produce a cruel despot, so can imbalance in administering drugs make you subject to bloody tyrants—submission, addiction, and death. Here the devil is in the imbalance, not the details.

The principle of DRP goes well beyond drugs and medication. And it's not just in the realm of government that we can draw a parallel. Any activity we engage in is subject to the strict balance of dosage, regimen, and protocol. Everything, from the food we eat to the pleasures we pursue and the work we perform, should be measured according to how much (dosage), when (regimen), and how (protocol). It always comes down to DRP. Maintaining a proper balance of the three is the key to a healthy life.

In our highly specialized culture, people in pursuit of professional excellence can easily extend themselves too far in just one direction and lose their balance. They are like scientists who specialize, so to speak, in the left quadrant of the right nostril. Narrowly specialized people remind me of someone trying to walk a high wire. It doesn't take much for them to topple—the higher and narrower the specialty, the greater the fall. Many people fail in life because they major in minor things.

Truly creative people, on the other hand, see and think more broadly—beyond black and white, this or that, up or down, and exercise a generalist's healthy curiosity in everything. They apply knowledge, form, and function from one field to another—mixing, balancing, synthesizing. The genius, often seen as odd or eccentric, has the same number of brain cells, but those cells burn brighter, deeper, and longer. Make full use of your own inherent creative gifts. Follow the command of Jesus: "Let your light so shine before men, that they may see your good works" (Matt. 5:16).

The Big Picture

I have found that fresh ideas in any area of life usually come from outside the defined alternatives. For example, during the uranium boom of the fifties, everyone was scurrying around buying shares and hoping they'd keep skyrocketing. Uranium stock companies were springing up faster than you could say "atomic energy." People expected to strike it rich, just as they do today with Internet stocks. Instead of playing the game the way everyone else was, I looked outside the box of defined alternatives to find the better way.

At the time, I was making sales calls for the Upjohn Company at the University of Utah Medical Center. When I finished talking to the doctors, I'd wander over to the mining and geology departments and chat about uranium with Alex Oblad and other professors. Then, when I was downtown, I'd drop in at the mining assay offices on West Temple to look at some of the so-called "hot rocks" and learn where they could be found.

Seeing the bigger picture, I started staking uranium claims on public lands. I'd watch for claims of hot rocks to be verified, then I'd stake claims on adjacent lands all over southeastern Utah and southwestern Colorado and Wyoming. Looking at the bigger picture also meant enlisting energies beyond my own and developing a system that extended my control over the uranium market. I showed maps to other drug salesmen who made calls in territories where uranium had been found. I paid them $50 cash for staking claims in my name when they traveled through the uranium-rich areas. It was a good deal for them because all they had to do was go out and pound a stake into the ground.

Later, the claims usually sold to the penny stock promoters for $3,000 to $6,000 each. My investment was rarely more than a modest claim-filing fee and the $50 commission to a salesman friend. But I never promoted the stock, never sat on the companies' boards of directors, and I always sold as soon as my investment or stock option had doubled.

I profited by looking at the big picture and adding the third dimension. I applied this same principle to medical monitoring and diagnostic devices. Most recently I've applied the principle to technology for global communication. Looking at the bigger picture is seeing the forest instead of the trees, traveling not a narrow path but exploring the entire landscape. Looking for the third dimension gives the mind room to expand, places to ponder, and scope to find the better way.

2

THE MAGIC
OF THREE

∾o∾

I'm fascinated by how often things are structured in threes and how often three is the magic number. The matter that makes up our visible world has a basic three-part structure: protons, neutrons, and electrons are poised in a precise three-dimensional dance to form atomic particles.

What I find especially interesting, and even elegant, is that protons and neutrons are constructed in a three-way balance of tiny particles called quarks, which can be either positive or negative. Each proton contains three quarks, and each quark has a three-part charge. A proton, for example, contains two quarks with a 2/3 unit of positive charge and one quark with a 1/3 unit of negative charge. A neutron is neutral because the three quarks it contains cancel out their positive and negative charges. Two quarks have a 1/3 negative charge, and the third quark carries a 2/3 positive charge.

This calibrated precision of matter in our physical world is apparently balanced by what physicists call "antimatter," particles that are the exact duplicates of visible atomic particles, with an equal but opposite electrical charge. There's a theory that atoms of antimatter could combine to create antimatter objects, maybe even antimatter worlds populated with antimatter people. There's even a hypothesis that our visible universe might be balanced in some way by an invisible universe of antimatter stars and galaxies. Not long ago, a satellite detected an antimatter cloud bubbling up from the center of our galaxy. It's like a big fountain spewing particles 3,000 light years into space.

Scientists have never actually seen antimatter particles. They know something is there, however, because when an ordinary electron meets up with an antimatter positron, they vaporize each other, producing pure energy in the form of light 250,000 times that of ordinary light. This is a perfect example of two things coming together to produce a third. In our universe, three is always the lowest common denominator.

As we learn more about the DNA molecule that carries our genetic information, we see the power of tripartite form. It has always seemed to me that the double helix might not give the full picture of DNA, or do justice to its dimensional complexity. So I'm not surprised that scientists have recently claimed to see a

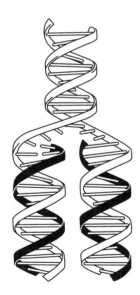

Figure 9– Double Strand Helix in Process of Replication

third strand in some DNA sequences. It's fitting that this third strand appears to play a balancing function in gene development.

Biologists are now realizing that each living thing is shaped by a complex interplay of genes and environment. An organism is not a passive passenger through its environment, but is an active traveler, selecting and "constructing" its environment in subtle but significant ways. Plants shape themselves to fit different circumstances, creating a distinctive environment. We, too, shape and construct environments as we learn, grow, and mature. We are formed from our inherited genes—approximately 40,000 from mother, 40,000 from father—to interact with our given environments. Once again, a basic triad is the animating force behind the balance of the very essence of life: genes, environment, organism. These three form a metaphorical "triple helix" that make up and balance our human essence.

Even the food we eat is structured by the triad of carbohydrates, protein, and fats. Our patterns of eating fall naturally into a three-part rhythm: most cultures dine three times a day.

The structure of language itself, the syntax we use to communicate meaning, at its most basic level is a three-part structure: subject, verb, object. Take the example of the most simple and profound sentence in our language: "God created the world." God (subject) created (verb) the world (object).

The ability to recognize a three-part structure seems to be innate, a basic gift of the human mind. Seven-month-old babies are able to recognize different combinations of three syllables in "sentences" devised by developmental psychologists. For instance, babies can distinguish and respond to a three-part pattern such as "li ti ti" or "wo fe wo" embedded in a recording of random sounds. When my kids were babies I noticed something similar—their "baby talk" had the rhythms of regular sentences.

This innate ability to respond to pattern and rhythm

accounts for the great power of music, which is a kind of inter-national language. It, too, can be defined in terms of three elements—melody, harmony, and rhythm. A common form of musical rhythm is the three-beat meter. Jazz gets its distinctive "swing" rhythm from improvising within the three-beat struc-ture. Melody is similarly structured in three parts. One melodic formula consists of an opening 16 bars, an 8-bar bridge, and a final 8-bar reprise. The opening 16 bars are an 8 plus 8 repeti-tion, which sets up the 8-bar bridge, followed by a return to the opening melody.

Harmony, the third basic component of music, creates our sense of musical dimension. The basic harmonic structure of music is the triad chord, consisting of the root, the third, and the fifth tones of the scale. Such is the power of triadic form that playing just the root and fifth tone will leave an attentive listener with an impression of the third tone.

The magic of three is basic to how we experience and describe time—past, present, and future. A single event is dis-tinguished as such because it has a beginning, middle, and end. Space is also conceived as three-dimensional, having height, width, and depth.

Enumerating in basic threes is a simple and convenient way to keep track of things and establish a rudimentary order. But we should go beyond simple threes and think creatively about the three-dimensional creation of all things. "Dimension" is the key concept to problem solving. Check to see if you have only one or two concepts, then find the third dimension, not just the third in a series.

The magic of three operates in a truly "magical" way when the first two concepts in a series come together to suggest a third idea. This cumulative power of two coming together to produce a third is, of course, the principle of creation: one man and one woman come together to create a child. But even on a linguistic level we can see how two words somehow combine, perhaps in a "conceptual synergy," to yield a third meaning. Thus honor and love lead to obedience. Faith and gratitude find expression in spoken testimony. And Jesus, whose admonitions and parables rely on the magic of three, told us that the way and the truth equal eternal life.

Basic Triads

The basic triad of life is God, self, and others. I need God, I need me, and I need others. We balance each of these dimensions as God has so precisely, so delicately, and so tenderly balanced our creation, our environment, and our life. For many people, God may be the lost dimension. A person may try to build a life without God and manage to do it to some extent. But such a person is like someone who refuses to acknowledge the third dimension—he sentences himself to living a flat life in a round world.

The most fundamental and intimate triad in life is mother, father, and child. We all begin life as the weakest member of this triangle, and in essential ways, we are all shaped by this dynamic three-way relationship. As I've grown older, I see more and more how I was shaped by my parents. I've already described how they taught me lessons in balance, each in their own way—Dad by insisting on rhythm and pace, and Mother by emphasizing the danger of going to extremes.

But they shaped me in many small ways, too. I sometimes catch a glimpse of myself in a mirror making a hand gesture or some body movement and feel that I'm looking at Dad. And sometimes I'll catch myself behaving in a particular way and realize that I'm doing something Dad used to do. Even my voice sometimes sounds so much like his that it startles me.

I'm also aware of things I've picked up from Mother. She had a playful sense of humor that allowed her and Dad to engage in friendly teasing. I'll find myself in this same sort of game with my family, teasing them about this and that. We can kid each other and laugh together.

Little things like that prove to me how we are shaped in ways great and small by our parents. The triad of mother, father, and child is the best evidence of the synergy that is the basis of life—two things coming together to produce a third. One (father) and one (mother) equal three (child). Furthermore, we must witness at least three generations to establish a meaning-ful pedigree chart with our DNA genealogy. The Bible repre-sents this vividly with Abraham, Isaac, and Jacob.

The human gestation period is divided into trimesters, not just for convenience but because each trimester represents dis-tinct stages of growth. During the first three months, the fetus achieves noticeable human form. During the second three months, the baby begins to move—called "quickening." In the final three months, the baby reaches the stage of being able to breathe, cry, and eat in the world outside the womb. Gestation is itself an element in the tripartite process that begins with conception and ends with birth.

Basic Spiritual Structures

Theologies basically structure experience in terms of three. Judaism postulates three conditions for repentance: remorse, confession, and resolution. Jewish scripture consists of The Law, The Prophets, and The Writings. The interlocked triangles of the Star of David recognize the insistent three-dimensional nature of the created world.

Figure 10– The Star of David

Islam had its beginnings when Muhammad heard the voice of Allah command him three times to preach the existence of the one and only God. In Muslim prayers, Allah is addressed in praises of three: "All Merciful, All Knowing, All Loving," and "Helper of the afflicted, Reliever of all distress, and Consoler of the broken-hearted." As in Judaism and Christianity, Islam worships God as the third dimension of being. This is made clear in the story of Muhammad and a companion hiding in a cave from enemies. When the companion despaired of their safety, saying, "We are but two," Muhammad answered, "Nay, we are three, for God is with us."

Eastern religion is also structured in terms of three. Buddhism describes the three aspects of the Buddha and instructs followers to eliminate the three evils of anger, greed, and ignorance. Hinduism worships three deities: Brahma, Vishnu, and Shiva. Polynesian religions draw a three-dimensional picture of the world: Nature, Divinity, and Human Beings. At the core of Christianity is the trinity of Father, Son, and Holy Ghost.

Judaism and Christianity posit three essential spiritual elements. Jews emphasize faith, hope, and purity, which parallel the Christian virtues of faith, hope, and charity. St. Paul, the apostle of action, embodied these virtues. I especially like him because he emphasized the need to act as well as to hope and believe. "Faith, hope, and charity" is a more eloquent formulation of a triad central to my philosophy of balance: Think (Hope), Feel (Faith), Do (Charity).

In the New Testament, the Transfiguration is structured by threes. Jesus leads his three chief disciples—Peter, James, and John—to the top of Mount Hermon. According to some accounts, the three disciples hear a compelling voice say three times, "This is my son." Then the disciples behold three figures above them: Moses, Elijah, and in the middle, Jesus, attired in robes shining white. The triplicate vision emphasizes the power, mystery, and glory of the moment.

The Crucifixion enacts a powerful image of the three-dimensional nature of creation. Christ on the cross stretches his arms toward the two thieves, an emblem of how his divine nature is balanced by his human incarnation. Christ's redemption of mankind is suggested by the cross pointing heavenward. "Today shalt thou be with me in paradise" (Luke 23:43), said Jesus to the thief. Paradise is the third dimension that balances the human and the divine.

In The Church of Jesus Christ of Latter-day Saints the principle of three operates theologically and organizationally. Joseph Smith, the founder and designated first prophet, seer, and revelator of the LDS church, constantly revealed and confirmed the three-dimensional nature of all other things theologically. One night a messenger from God's presence came to Joseph Smith three times before the cock crowed, to instruct him as to the bringing forth of the Book of Mormon. Latter-day Saint theology also posits three levels of salvation: celestial, terrestrial, and telestial. Furthermore, to the traditional notion of this world and the next, the dogma posits a third dimension—a premortal existence.

Mormon missionaries preach the gospel two by two, but the Holy Spirit is a third companion walking with them. The mission statement of the LDS church is three-fold: *teach* the gospel, *perfect* the members, and *perform* temple ordinances for the dead. When temples are dedicated, the congregation joins together in the "Hosanna Shout": three times the congregation exclaims "Hosanna, hosanna, hosanna, to God and the Lamb."

A powerful LDS triad is teach, redeem, strengthen. This is of paramount importance in parenting. Parents carefully teach, continually redeem, and ideally strengthen their children spiritually, intellectually, and physically. LDS teachings recognize and promote the family in building knowledge, fostering understanding, and creating love.

Organizationally, the LDS church recognizes the fundamental principle of three in the First Presidency, stake leadership, ward bishoprics, and the presidencies of auxiliary organizations. Besides the Bible, there are three LDS books of scripture: The Book of Mormon, The Doctrine and Covenants, and The Pearl of Great Price.

Triads and Temples

The principle of three is essential to the Jewish belief about the temple in Jerusalem. The Wailing Wall is all that remains of the Second Temple, destroyed in 70 A.D. The First Temple had been built on the same spot, selected by Solomon because it was a place where God was believed to have stopped a plague. Jewish scripture teaches that after the destruction of the first two temples, Messiah will come and the Third Temple will be built.

The temple is central to Judaism and other religions because it is seen as God's dwelling place on earth and the ultimate source of spirituality. The symbolism of the temple is evident in the very word itself, which comes from the Latin word for *time.* In the temple, rituals are performed at sacred times, and these rituals remind us of the inherent rhythms, central events, and eternal nature of life.

Time is a meaningful concept in LDS temple ceremonies. Baptisms for the dead, temple marriages, and family sealings reach into the past, celebrate the present, and look to the future. Temples are therefore places not only to redeem the dead but also to renew the living. In LDS temples, as in cathedrals and other sacred places, time is expanded to remind us of the eternal nature of all things.

When I visited Japan, I was impressed by how their Zen temple gardens suggest this same sense of eternity. Their gardens are different from ours: instead of lush vegetation and intricate arrangements of flowers, the temple gardens consist of raked gravel wavelets and carefully placed stones. The wavelets denote streaming life, and the stones symbolize timeless stability.

The most basic stone formation is called Sanzon, or the Buddha Three, with three stones sitting on a field of the rippled gravel. The central, rising vertical stone is flanked and supported by two horizontal stones. The arrangement of three stones gives you a sense of aspiration and stability, both of which are components of what I call True Balance.

The most famous of the Zen temple gardens is Ryoan-ji in Kyoto, Japan. It's a rectangle the size of a squash court. But the patterned sand and the 15 stones—arranged in groups of 7, 5, and 3—convey a powerful sense of sacred space. The simple garden leads you through three dimensions to meditate on the expanse of eternity.

The temple gardens of Japan, like LDS and Jewish temples, Muslim mosques, and Catholic cathedrals, offer a sacred space outside our ordinary material world. They encourage us to meditate on essential and eternal things. The triadic configuration of the temple gardens—the immaculate surrounding grounds, the simple temple, the holy sanctum—reminds us of the full dimension of our existence.

Japanese tea gardens also fulfill a sacred function, and it struck me that the tea ceremonies parallel endowment ceremonies performed in LDS temples. The particular details are not as important as the larger structure and significance of the experience. Both the garden and temple ceremonies are organized into different stages: in the tea garden, there is a preliminary gathering at a waiting bench, then a walk along stepping stones, a cleansing ritual, then entry through a low door (to encourage humility) into the enclosed pavilion.

In LDS temple endowment ceremonies, worshipers advance through the Garden Room, the Telestial Room, and the Terrestrial Room. Then the participants enter the Celestial

Room through a veil, which is a similitude of the veils in the tabernacle of Moses and the temple of Solomon. Passage into the Celestial Room symbolizes passage into the presence of God.

Our Three-Structured Brain

It is significant that our brain, our very means of apprehending, encountering, and shaping the world, has a three-part structure. Research by Dr. Paul McLean suggests that the human brain has three layers, each functioning differently and controlling specific activities:

1. The R-complex is concerned with survival of the individual and the preservation of the species. It operates by instinct and repetition, driving us to create shelter, choose a mate, and defend the nest.

2. The limbic system is responsible for our "gut reaction" to things and alerts us to danger. It operates through the senses to give us information about our environment. When you smell rotten meat and gag, the limbic system is at work. Emotion, which is the physical reaction of the body to sense information, is also the product of the limbic system. Basic emotions such as fear and aggression help us survive hostile environments.

3. The neocortex does our abstract thinking. It takes in information though the five senses, like the limbic system, but it doesn't produce physical responses. Nor is it focused so much on preservation, like the R-complex. The neocortex sorts sensory data into categories, makes connections, and sets up comparisons. It allows us to store information so we can remember things, draw conclusions about our experience, and make predictions about the future. Language, art, and culture are all creations of the neocortex.

But there's another way of looking at the brain that's instructive for my idea of balance. It is what the neuroscientists call hemispheric synchronization. Left and right hemispheres of the brain combine signals to create a new perceptual dimension. This happens with sight, sound, and thought. Our eyes, for instance, receive sensory data from slightly different angles, creating a triangle with the perceived object:

Figure 11– Visual Perception

Our brain then synchronizes the visual data into a stereoscopic perception of the external world.

Our ears, similarly, form a triangle with the source and transmit slightly different audio signals to their corresponding hemisphere.

Figure 12– Auditory Perception

These signals are then synchronized to give us a "third" sound. What's fascinating to me is that this synchronizing of sight and sound with thought is a truly "new" dimension. Two things again come together to produce a third. The workings of our sensory apparatus teach us to apply the same process in our own life. Find the third dimension of any situation, problem, or challenge for more accurate location and precise awareness.

An example from the animal world offers an instructive analogy on the power of the third dimension. Cows digest food by regurgitating and rechewing their food as it makes its way through a system of three stomachs. As unappetizing as this sounds, it illustrates the idea of "chewing" on our ideas, developing them as we ruminate and work them over. To ruminate, interestingly, means both to "chew over" and to ponder, consider, and entertain ideas. So remind yourself to use the same process with your ideas. Don't gulp them down like fast food; chew your ideas at least three times to really learn, know, and understand.

Three's the Charm

The magic of three dimensions animates cultural institutions and helps us make sense of our experience. It's no coincidence that the three-act structure of a play, the most immediate "imitation of life," has endured for hundreds of years. Three acts are needed to show the full dimension of human actions—cause, effect, and consequence. Nursery rhymes, education, myths, religions, commerce, even aphorisms and jokes, all utilize the principle of three to generate real meaning.

Nursery rhymes are full of threes: three blind mice, three men in a tub, three bags full. In fairy tales the king has three sons, the wicked stepmother has three daughters. The Brothers Grimm collected countless stories with three central characters: Three Little Men in the Woods, Three Spinners, Three Snake Leaves. Goldilocks confronts three bears, and the Three Little Pigs build three different houses. The hero of a tale usually has to suffer three tests or undertake three journeys.

There is the Bible story in which Nebuchadnezzar throws Shadrach, Meshach, and Abednego into the fiery furnace because they are loyal to their God and won't bow down to the golden idol. Nebuchadnezzar does a turnabout when the three Jews are unscathed by the fire, and he commands that his people worship the God of Shadrach, Meshach, and Abednego. The story is more complete, powerful, and persuasive with three characters rather than just one or two, which wouldn't be enough to suggest the strength and extent of the Jewish faith. And even the rhythm of the three names—Shadrach, Meshach, and Abednego—sticks in your memory so you remember the message of the story.

In the same vein, I think about the Book of Mormon account of the three Nephites, who were promised they would tarry on the earth until the return of Jesus Christ. The theme of three is also powerfully exemplified in the three wise men, bearing three gifts to the baby Jesus.

Another story in the Bible uses the principle of three to teach a profound lesson about personal salvation: the prodigal son returns home to the welcoming arms of his father. The good son, who stayed home, wonders at the father's generosity. What is the lesson? The father and the two sons can be interpreted as representing three parts of the individual soul that must be reunited if we are to become whole persons. The father is the source of life, and both the good and the prodigal parts of ourselves must be embraced by the source of our being.

In classical mythology, the universe is divided among three brothers: Zeus is lord of the sky, Poseidon rules the sea, and Hades presides over the underworld. The Three Graces are Aglaia (Splendor), Euphrosyne (Mirth), and Thalia (Good Cheer). Three-winged, dragon-like creatures called Gorgons had three sisters—gray women known as The Graiae. Then there were the Three Fates: Clotho, the spinner who spins the thread of life; Lachesis, who assigns one's destiny; and Atropos, who wields the shears that cut the thread of life.

Education has traditionally been structured by the principle of three. Schooling in the Middle Ages began with the Trivium (the Latin term for the intersection of three roads): grammar, logic, and rhetoric. Today we divide lower education into elementary, middle, and high school institutions. The residue of the medieval structure is revealed when we call elementary "grammar" school. The triadic structure also manifests itself in higher education where graduates can advance through three degrees: bachelor, master, and doctorate.

Many games and sports are organized by the principle of three. Take baseball, for example: three strikes, and you're out; three outs in an inning; and three times three equals nine innings—a complete game. The goal of the game is to get around all three bases and come home. Something about that goal resonates in our collective psyche—first base, second base, third base, and finally—coming home.

In the sphere of government, the success of the United States system lies in the genius of three basic branches of government—the legislative, the executive, and the judicial. These three branches must remain in delicate balance to preserve our American ideals. When overriding power resides in one element—whether executive, legislative, or judicial—tyranny is inevitable. A government consisting of two parts is vulnerable to deadlock and perpetual conflict, each side warring against the other. Our three-branch system tolerates conflict but prevents power-grabs. It insists on the kind of interaction and dialogue needed for dynamic balance and self-renewing stability.

In the rule of law and the development of government, history shows us that there are essentially three ways to order a society: tyranny, anarchy, and democracy. Tyranny represents total obedience; anarchy—total freedom; and democracy—the rule of law. Anarchy was the original state of nature; tyranny was a reaction to a lawless society. A strong figure can seize power and impose his will on a group eager for order at any cost. The only viable alternative to anarchy or tyranny is democracy—the law of the people.

Pure democracy is threatened by tyranny of the majority. Representative democracy—a republic—safeguards the vulnerable minority from a majority quick to impose its will. In tyranny, the ruler imposes his will and his law upon the people; in anarchy, each person is a law unto himself. Only in a democracy—the law of the people—is the law beyond the whim of any individual, tyrant, or anarchist. That's why the principle of "no one above the law" is such a profound idea. The law is a "third way," a most delicately and precisely balanced ground that is also "below" everyone. Only democracy has a balanced three-dimensional foundation upon which everyone can securely stand.

The Structure of Business Success

The principle of three also works in business. A successful business will stimulate creativity, build a sense of community, and encourage practical action. Business must balance individual creativity and group effort on the fulcrum of pragmatism. The private business corporation puts ideas into practice by balancing individual initiative and community purpose.

A successful commercial enterprise must continually balance ideas, people, and capital. If you have a great idea but few skilled people or limited capital, you're out of balance. Another essential triad in business is assets, liabilities, and capital. If just one element is ignored, you're out of business.

Managers often get out of balance when dealing with subordinates; they neglect one or more elements of another fundamental triad: instruction, responsibility, and authority. It's amazing to me how often one or two of these elements are withheld. Many middle managers are given responsibility but no authority. They are stymied by a boss who hangs on to authority like a miser hoarding his treasure. Authority that isn't "spent" is as useless as a bag of coins hidden under a mattress. Instruction is essential, too. You can be given responsibility and authority, but unless you know what you're about, you are as powerless as a person shopping with "play money."

Successful Selling

Three elements fundamental to successful selling are knowledge, imagination, and evaluation. You need to know your product, you need imagination to market your product, and finally, you need judgment to evaluate the chance for success.

To close the sale, the salesman orchestrates another triad: 1) the opening that gets attention, 2) the body that provides information, and 3) the conclusion that asks for and makes the sale. It's somewhat like the Southern preacher who stated this formula for giving a successful sermon: "I tell 'em what I'm gonna' tell 'em, then I tell 'em, and then I tell 'em what I've told 'em."

Selling and proselytizing are similar. The three steps of conversion are: discussion, testimony, and baptism. In introducing and selling a new technology, the three equivalent stages are: instruction, demonstration, and application.

The successful salesman employs three elements: "think, tell, and do." Many great ideas fail because the salesperson lacks the ability or persistence to *tell* customers about the product. But the salesperson who only *thinks* and *tells* will not succeed. You must also *do*. You ask for the order, close the loop, and make the sale.

In closing the deal, timing is critical. Sometimes you have to force the issue, as we did when we sold a company of ours called Sorex. Two companies were interested in acquiring Sorex but were reluctant to make a commitment. We finally gave them a deadline, asking them to decide one way or another within a week. That brought the matter to a head. One company dropped out, and we made a better arrangement with the other.

Know When to Act

The essence of timing is knowing when to act. Sometimes you play the predator and "move in for the kill." Other times you nurture a deal as if it were a delicate plant, allowing it to blossom in its own time. "Ripeness is all," said Shakespeare. Don't strip green apples from trees.

Auctions, in particular, demand quick and decisive strikes. Several years ago the Union Pacific Railroad held an auction to sell land and properties around Rock Springs, Wyoming. I had never seen the land, but I could tell by studying the map and looking at patterns of growth that the properties were promising. So I immediately bought seventy-seven acres, sight unseen, for $40,000.

Within a month I had an offer of $80,000 for the acreage—not a bad return in just thirty days! But my intuition told me not to sell yet. Three years later, I sold seven of those acres for $287,000 and retained the continuing appreciation on the remaining seventy. Again, it came down to timing, or more precisely, the delicate balancing of time, energy, and motion (T.E.M.). In this case, *energy* was represented by growth patterns, *motion* consisted of the lines of development, and *time* determined when it was ripe to buy and when to sell.

Educate Your Intuition

Another triad essential for success in business (and in life) is optimism, reality, and intuition. I refuse to get too optimistic if the research and facts seem good but my feelings are negative. Blind optimism is sheer folly. All the positive attitude in the world won't ensure success if facts or intuition are working against you. Don't misunderstand, optimism is wonderful, but only when it is married to logic and reality. Even when the facts are in your favor, consult your intuition. If you have an uneasy feeling about something, you probably ought to take a second and a third look at it. Cultivate a positive and educated attitude—"expectant of good"—but also consult contrary intuitions.

Intuition means weighing all your experience against the current reality. When there's a "fit" between reality and intuition, you have a basis for optimism. It's another case of two things coming together to produce a third—reality plus intuition equals optimism. Optimism provides the stimulus to take not just a calculated but a calibrated risk.

When I've ignored my intuition—that feeling which is the sum of who you are—I have lost my balance and no longer been the master of my fate. When I have given things, but not myself, I've felt as though I'm just going through the motions. But I have never lost when I've committed myself fully and sincerely. It's like balancing your checkbook. Unless sincerity is your beginning balance, all the other numbers will be lies. Errors multiply until your "personal account" is in a hopeless muddle. You lose a sure, confident, and balanced sense of yourself.

To become someone others will believe in, you must first believe in yourself. Faith in yourself is a mental medicine with no contraindications. Within you await wonderful and powerful answers. When you listen to your intuitions, when you look within for answers, your life becomes what you want it to be. Don't limit yourself, and don't leave answers to chance. If you take time to wish upon a star, your dream can become a waking reality.

You are then on your own unique, God-given errand. As Oprah Winfrey has said, "God can dream a bigger dream for you than you can ever dream for yourself." Don't ever forget how special you are. As you succeed, you will experience a new euphoria and joy—a "high" that will propel you ever onward and upward.

Here's a list of informal principles or "rules of thumb" I give people on my sales staff. I think they apply to most situations in life.

Don't Wait

- The Golden Rule: Treat customers the way you want to be treated. The Platinum Rule: Treat customers the way they want to be treated. The New Rule: Treat customers as if you were the customer!
- A prospect must buy you before he buys your product.
- You can't just sell products. You have to sell services, benefits, and solutions. Most of all, you sell yourself.
- Before I can sell something to a particular customer, I must see the world through that customer's eyes.
- You make the sale when the prospect understands that it will cost more to do nothing about the problem than to do something about it.
- One of the worst mistakes you can make is to think you are working for someone else.
- Your attitude will defeat you faster than your competition.
- Of all the things you wear, your expression is the most important.
- Killing time murders opportunities.
- Digging for facts is smarter than jumping to conclusions.
- The secret of success is tenacity.
- The line between failure and success is so fine that we scarcely know when we pass it, so fine that we are often on the line and do not know it.
- Do it. Do it right. Do it right now!

3

TRIADS AND THE
TEST OF TRUTH

∽◦∾

The power of three sustains our sense of reality and confirms our apprehension of truth. Consider the common practice of using examples to prove a proposition or win an argument. You often hear someone defend a position by saying, "Well, that doesn't prove anything. That's just one example." Even two examples are often not enough because two instances of some generalization can be explained away as coincidence.

Three examples thus become the minimum "proof" of any assertion. Three witnesses are needed to establish credibility. Three letters of recommendation are often required for a job application. A quorum of at least three is usually necessary to take an official action or make a valid transaction.

This power of three as a kind of "proof" is also present in popular folklore and cultural "rules of thumb." Three is the standard that signals both failure and success. Three instances establish the reality of a situation—good or bad. There were three wise men bearing three gifts. Jesus was denied three times by Peter. "Three strikes and you're out" is a common standard for failure in any number of situations, ranging from criminal convictions to the dating game. People talk about a drowning person "going under for the third time." According to Ben Franklin, "Both fish and visitors begin to stink in three days."

On the other hand, the principle of three also serves to measure and prove success: Three coins in a fountain; knock three times on the ceiling if you love me; the third time's the charm. In the New Testament, the power of three is emphasized throughout. For instance, Jesus in the wilderness is tempted three times by Satan, and three times he resists him. Jesus rises on the third day, and we are promised that "in the third day he will raise us up, and we shall live in his sight" (Hosea 6:2).

Complete the Triangle

The power of three gives life to basic forms. Consider the triangle. A minimum of three lines is necessary to make a structure that has content. You need three straight lines to contain or enclose an area. You can see the power of the triangle to make sense of flat, two-dimensional space.

Let's use straight lines to illustrate the point. Draw a straight line such as:

Figure 13– Straight Line

The single line is meaningless. Add a second line to create an angle such as:

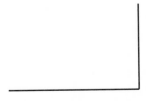

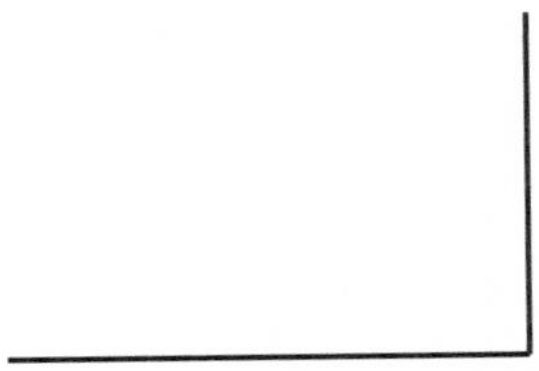

Figure 14– Right Angle

and the possibility of form begins to emerge.

But only when a third line creates a triangle do you have a complete and coherent structure:

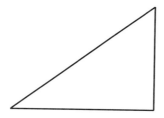

Figure 15– The Completed Triangle

This shows the importance of always going beyond one or two possibilities. A third "line" is necessary to make whole any formation or situation.

Regardless of the situation, we have an itch to complete the triangle; when we're presented with just two sides of a situation, we have an uneasy feeling that something is missing. Language, culture, or theology may offer us only two alternatives, two sides of the triangle. We therefore must complete the triangle to illuminate specific situations and enrich our perception of the "big picture." Completing the triangle enables us to better understand the ways and means of God's creation. It gives us insight into who we are, the laws by which we are created, and how we, too, become creators.

Completing the triangle has another instructive aspect. Consider two lines forming a right angle, AB and BC:

Figure 16– Second Aspect of the Triangle

Conventional two-dimensional and dualistic perception dictates that you follow the established lines if you want to get from A to C. Think of AB and BC as well-worn trails in a field—routes that hikers automatically follow.

It may well be that the best route from A to C is through point B. But geometry (the square of the hypotenuse is equal to the sum of the squares of the sides of a right triangle) tells us that the hypotenuse from A to C is a much shorter distance:

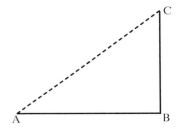

Figure 17– The Hypotenuse of the Triangle

Sometimes, therefore, you must strike out across an unmarked field, creating your own hypotenuse. This is another way of "completing the triangle."

Completing the triangle is a schematic way of how we find the third dimension. We can also talk about "completing the circle" as a way of structuring and giving form to experience. The curve of an uncompleted arc "points the way" to completion, just as a partial moon gives promise of a full moon:

Figure 18– Completing the Circle

The habit of drawing that third line, of discovering the third dimension, will put you in touch with your natural propensity to complete the picture. In addition to helping you make sense of any situation, looking for the third dimension kick starts your creativity, expands your imagination, and enhances your ability to find the better way.

Learning to See

Seeing in three dimensions is natural. But it is "autonomic"—not "automatic." The ability develops naturally during the early months of life. As we move about and enlarge our understanding of our environment, we must *learn* to see the world in three dimensions. I noted earlier how our eyes synchronize to produce our stereoscopic perception of the world. But the brain has to learn how to put different visual signals together to create a third signal that provides depth perception.

That we "learn" to see has been shown in the cases of blind people who have gained their sight through cataract surgery. The world looks strange to these people after surgery—a jumble of light and color. For a time, they have no sense of dimension or depth, no real conception of height or distance. A house a mile away seems nearby. Nor do these people have any sense of size. When one of them, a young girl, was asked how big her mother was, she held her thumb and index finger a few inches apart.

Just as we must learn how to perceive our world three-dimensionally, so too we must learn to use all our God-given senses to represent the world in three dimensions. When kids draw pictures, they make their trees or houses or people as flat as the paper they draw on. Most people never learn to draw in three dimensions. It takes an innovative mind, an artistic eye, and a trained hand to render the world in height, width, and depth. In the history of art, the ability to render the world in three dimensions is a relatively recent development.

The Egyptians, for example, limited themselves to two dimensions when they rendered their deities on flat surfaces. Only their sculptural art is truly three-dimensional.

Figure 19– Two-dimensional Egyptian Art

Not until the Italian Renaissance do we see a significant change in how the world is represented. The fourteenth century painter Giotto found a way to see beyond the two dimensions of medieval mosaics and to present people in their rounded reality. This new way of "seeing" was central to the new humanism of the Renaissance. People began to see and think of themselves as full, three-dimensional, unique individuals.

What does the development of three-dimensional art have to teach us? When we perceive the world fully in the round, we increase our power to understand how the world works. More important, we increase our power to act with the moving world and make things better. Innovation becomes second nature. Unless we see the endless possibilities of our three-dimensional world, we are no better than those primitive artists trapped in the flat landscape of their black and white stick figures.

Find the Third Dimension

When you learn to think three-dimensionally, you'll see that even so-called "empty space" isn't really empty. Instead, it is buzzing and brimming with possibility and potential. To the Western mind, empty space is too often considered as nothingness, an insignificant void. This attitude shows up in Western art by the need to fill every inch of canvas with shape and color. Asian art is different. Look at a Japanese painting, and you'll be struck by how much white space there is. The "empty spaces" in the picture invite your imagination to fill in and complete the painting, and your creative mind imparts a third dimension to the painting.

The ability to see new dimensions and new possibilities in empty space has practical applications. It's not a talent useful only in art appreciation. Filling in the empty space makes it possible to imagine the potential of any new territory. When I explore a piece of undeveloped land, I don't look upon it as a barren stretch of dirt, sagebrush, and scrub oak. I envision a landscape blossoming with buildings, homes, and neighborhoods.

Every situation teems with sparkling facets of possibility. If you're looking for that third dimension—that new possibility—you'll find a better way to do whatever you're doing. Balance is created by perceiving possibility. True Balance is therefore a dynamic, creative, and self-perpetuating principle. True Balance is the basis of invention and innovation.

Seeing new dimensions is like looking into a kaleidoscope. The triangular colored glass and mirrors of a kaleidoscope refract light to produce new patterns and startling symmetries.

To children a kaleidoscope is an instrument of magic. The shifting symmetries provide constantly changing vistas that appeal to their sense of wonder and their fascination with new ways of seeing (have you ever watched little kids "turning the world upside down" by bending over and looking back between their knees?).

Of course, all you need to do with a kaleidoscope is twist the end of a tube. In real life action and energy and imagination are required to perceive the third dimension. Persist and the world will yield rich new colors, patterns, and symmetries. The blankest canvas is alive with potential. The quietest room is loud with original music. The emptiest space is teeming with unbuilt palaces.

Look for the third dimension by asking what the primary elements are. In reality there are always at least three. If you have less than three, you've limited your comprehension and logic to black or white, this or that, up or down, in or out, more or less. You become a fifteenth-century sailor trying to navigate the globe with a medieval two-dimensional map.

We live in a three-dimensional world. Space is structured by height, width, depth. Time is structured by past, present, future. Energy manifests itself as field, particle, or wave. The elements are structured by solids, liquids, and gases. In every aspect of life, as with the three primary colors, we get myriad shades and hues.

The physiology of the human heart offers a vivid lesson on the power of the third dimension. If you look just at the surface, it appears that electrical impulses wash over the heart in swirling waves. In reality, those two-dimensional swirls are just the outward traces of electrical impulses that spiral throughout the entire structure of the heart. Looking at just the surface is like looking at one end of a scroll and seeing only the concentric edges of the rolled paper.

Professor James P. Keener, an authority on heart physiology, says, "To understand what's happening on the surface, we actu-ally have to think three-dimensionally." The three-dimensional spirals of electricity are the motivaing force of the rhythmic sys-tole and diastole of the beating heart, as it pumps and moves blood throughout the body. As in everything, dimension is the field for rhythm and motion, and all work together to keep life in True Balance.

The power of the third dimension is evident in the inter-relatedness of the different spheres of experience. By shifting perspective, we can look at balance in terms of space, energy, and time. Thus we have the triad: dimension is balance in space, motion is balance in energy, and rhythm is balance in time.

Think, Tell, Do

What I call "true action" also has three sequential con-stituents: thinking, telling, doing. Too many limit themselves to only one or two of the three. What we *think, tell,* and *do* affects the whole system that we share. People who merely think, live in a world of unrealized potential and mere speculation. Those who tell before they think lack the insight to act with purpose. Without conscious and considered reflection, they waste time and wander. Thinking comes first, but unless you follow up with tell and do, you only have vacant illusions, empty thoughts, and unfulfilled dreams. Ideas and talk accomplish nothing; they must be put into action. The act of doing is all-important.

Seek to establish a stable balance in thinking, telling, and doing. There are many ways of thinking, many ways of telling, many ways of doing. The crucial thing is to do each in the cor-rect order. Think before you tell; tell before you do; and be sure that doing always follows thinking and telling.

The progressive triad of thinking, telling, and doing is powerful because it re-enacts a biological process. Once a thought is formulated, the firing of neurons and the resultant neuro-chemical activity produce physical changes that we rec-ognize as emotions. These emotions create tension that seeks resolution through action. So there is a spontaneous movement from thought to feeling to action. The most fundamental example of this is thinking about food. Fantasizing about pizza or a sirloin steak will induce feelings of hunger that may, in turn, incite you to satisfy your appetite.

Notice a difference in the second term of the biological triad—feeling instead of telling. Achieve the best use of the natural biological process by transmitting the feeling into telling. Telling the emotion, giving it a name, makes you the master of the emotion. Make the feeling component explicit and active, or the thought behind it will dwindle and die.

Set the Stage, Shop the Options, Shed the Excess

There's another way of conceptualizing the triad of thinking, telling, doing. Again, it's a progressive three-part action that addresses the three-dimensional nature of all things. First you set the stage. Then you shop the options. Finally you shed the excess. Winston Churchill said much the same thing in a farewell speech: "The great business of life is to be, to do, to do without, and to depart."

Shedding the excess, giving away, and doing without can be hard to do. It's human nature to acquire and hang onto things. I've still got my dad's old suitcase in my bedroom. There's not much in it; I've reduced the contents to a lot of odds and ends and trinkets. But it's hard for me to even think about getting rid of them because there's an emotional attachment. The things may be worthless, but I keep them because they remind me of Dad. I guess I hang onto them because, for me, they aren't "excess." Excess, then, is the key word. Shedding the excess means constantly calibrating the value of things.

This three-stage process of setting the stage, shopping the

options, and shedding the excess corresponds to the three stages of life:

1. We come into this world inhaling, grasping, and consuming hungrily. This sets the stage for our growth and survival.

2. We grow up, we shop our options, and we choose our course in life. All the while, we are learning, knowing, and understanding. We make a living, accumulate wisdom, and claim our portion.

3. We age and die, releasing and shedding all our excess. Death is the release of our mortal life and the return to the total fulfillment of our spiritual existence. We all must make friends with death because we are all going to die.

But the inevitability of aging and death doesn't mean we acquiesce quietly or simply give up. We are made to get out there and make things happen. Wherever we are along our journey is our reality, and we must be completely aware of our environment and attend tenaciously to the present moment. Here's a poem of mine that expresses the need to fully appreciate and enjoy where we are:

> When I look down the twisting road I must travel,
> Trouble and pain seem impossible to unravel.
> My burdens are many, and tears blur the goal,
> Brave or bold, time soon takes its toll.
>
> When doubt and fear imprison the mind,
> It seems the light will never shine.
> Then from the Lord above I hear,
> "Child you are mine.
>
> "Don't look far ahead or behind,
> Just walk one mile at a time.
> Trust in Me from day to day,
> And enjoy each step of the way."

II
MOTION

4

ENERGY AND EQUILIBRIUM

⚮

True Balance is continual rhythmic motion in three dimensions. In the truest sense, balance is indivisible—you can't actually separate its constituents. It isn't like taking apart a bicycle where you can still recognize the handlebars, the seat, and the tires. When we analyze balance, we're isolating its various aspects to better understand it. When we look at balance in terms of space, we talk about dimension; when we look at balance in terms of energy, we talk about motion; when we look at balance in terms of time, we talk about rhythm. But each of these elements exists in the context of the other two. Motion, for instance, "happens" in both space and time. And, of course, motion must be embodied in a three-dimensional substance. There must be something that moves.

Physicists describe three basic motions—straight, helical, and circular. Alone and in combination, these motions are shaped by gravity as we move through the three-dimensional world. When we walk, for instance, our seemingly straight-ahead motion is actually helical. With gravity keeping us centered and balanced, our bodies advance serpentine-like through helical curves. On a smaller and larger scale, atoms and planets perform a circular dance in their swinging orbits. Everything in the great Chain of Being moves in exquisite True Balance.

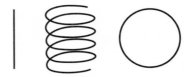

Figure 20– Three Types of Motion

The three basic motions, alone and in combination, operate in three dimensions and are defined by rhythm to constitute True Balance.

Life Is Motion

Everything—the very universe itself—is constantly in motion. The galaxies swirling through space, the planets orbiting the sun, electrons circling the nucleus of an atom, are all in perpetual motion. Motion alters and constantly renews the world, as some components hurry into existence and others fade away. We are renewed and reinvented every second, every minute, every hour. Molecules are modified, day and night come and go, seasons change.

Richard Feynman, the legendary physicist and Nobel laureate, argued that the most important scientific insight about our world is the atomic hypothesis, "All things are made of atoms, little particles that move around in perpetual motion, attracting each other when they are a little distance apart, but repelling upon being squeezed together." Something that appears to be totally inert, say a solid slab of marble, is really teeming with sub-atomic motion. In the world of organic matter, motion makes up the cycle of life. Seeds scatter, germinate, put down roots, blossom, bloom, decline, and die, but not before scattering more seeds to the wind to keep the cycle of life in constant motion.

Physicists have found that the motion of subatomic particles can be random and unpredictable. Even at the molecular level, motion can be random. Physicists call it Brownian Motion: microscopic particles suspended in a gas or liquid collide haphazardly with the molecules of the surrounding medium.

Exchange of Energy

Life is a thing in motion. For life to be sustained, for motion to continue, energy is required. When physicists talk about energy, they mean the ability to do work. That's not so different from what people mean when they use the word *energy* in ordinary conversation. People who have a lot of energy can do a lot of work.

Motion is always connected to energy; for where there is energy, there must also be motion. Conversely, where there is motion, there must be energy. But motion and energy are not the same thing. Energy is what makes motion possible. When something moves, it's evidence that energy is present.

What does this have to do with balance? Everything that happens, every event, is in some way an exchange of energy. Think of a rock rolling down a hill and hitting another rock or a billiard ball hitting another ball. Even buying a building or a piece of land is an exchange of energy. That exchange is an example of balance. Because motion is the consequence of energy, the energy exchange could be called balance in motion.

When I play squash, I become acutely conscious of balance in motion and the exchange of energy occurring all around me. I move my hand to toss the ball in the air and strike the ball with my racket, which imparts energy to the ball, which in turn exchanges energy with the surrounding walls as it angles and bounces before being struck by my opponent's racket. As I watch the ball dance and dart around the court, I sometimes imagine I'm at the center of an atom as electrons whirl and spin.

Figure 21– James L. Sorenson Playing Squash in 2000

Life, then, as a thing in *motion,* is a never-ending exchange of energy, a balance in motion. True economy in life is calibrating this exchange of *energy* wisely, not just consuming energy thoughtlessly, but using it wisely while it burns. The *time* of life is but a brief candle, soon extinguished. Time, energy, and motion. I referred to these three elements earlier when I was talking about buying land. But these three elements, T.E.M. (pronounced "teem"), are critical in all endeavors.

For me, the word "teem" has two meanings, which makes it a vivid reminder of the power of time, energy, and motion, as well as a realistic reminder that our time, energy, and motion all diminish as we age. Teem is a noun that denotes abundance, a cup running over. A drop of water teems with microorganisms, and the great globe of our world teems with multifarious life. Teem also is a verb that means to pour out or empty. When we put the two meanings of teem together, we become aware that one minute life is full and abundant, the next it's empty and at rest.

Remember the words of the rabbi? He said that we enter the world gasping for air, which is teeming with the very stuff of life, and depart the world as our last breath leaves our lips. We take nothing with us. We teem with life—time, energy, and motion—then life teems or pours out of us. We lose a little of life each minute, each hour, each day. Eventually mortal life ebbs away, leaving us at perfect peace and rest.

The Buddha said that the world is an ever-burning fire. Wisdom tells us that we should burn with a hard, gem-like flame because the more fire we have within us, the greater our capacity to warm others. Use your energy efficiently, so that your life will glow brighter, deeper, longer. In the Gospel of Thomas, Jesus says, "He who is near me is near the fire." Share your warmth and brighten the lives of others.

Balance on the Move

Balance may strike some as a static principle. They perceive balance as being the same as equilibrium, where active forces in our system cancel each other out, resulting in a condition that's motionless, quiet, and unchanging. In chemistry, for instance, equilibrium exists when forward and reverse reactions take place at the same rate. The chemical concentration of the reactants doesn't change with time. And in physics, equilibrium is achieved when the sum of the acting forces equals zero.

But the equilibrium in chemistry and physics is deceptive. Things are actually moving all the time. Chemical reactions don't come to a halt when equilibrium is achieved; the rate of the reactions simply becomes equalized.

True Balance lives in action. We see this when we emphasize "balance" as a verb rather than as a noun. A verb expresses motion, while a noun names an object, condition, or state of being. Consider the skier racing down a mountain. Delicate calibrations are necessary to maintain balance. The skier moves through all three dimensions, traversing the slope in rhythmic turns. The skier's balance is not static but dynamic. True Balance is not a product, posture, or place. True Balance is a process.

Finding Your Balance

A time comes in the process of balancing when action seems to cease, when everything apparently pauses at the point of perfect equilibrium. A diver poises at the edge of a springboard, everything gathered into a focused moment of stillness. But that stillness is really the point where motion merely changes direction, like a pendulum at the precise moment before it reverses its direction. From the first instant that a diver sets foot on the springboard, she never really stops moving. She is continually making tiny, almost imperceptible adjustments. She is re-calibrating in millisecond increments until everything is in balance. At the precise moment—she leaps!

The leap is not really a new motion but the consequence of everything coming into balance. In the necessary rhythm of balance in motion, the diver will calibrate her position before

Figure 22– The Balance of the Diver

entering the water. The diver who fails to maintain balance throughout the twists and turns of the dive will enter the water with a big belly flop. The conclusion of the dive, the entry into the water, is a consequence of the diver's calibrated balance on the springboard.

Attaining and retaining True Balance is necessary in all physical endeavors. Great athletes are good models because they have fine-tuned their inherent talents. Their bodies are instruments of balance in motion. I've used the diver as a model of True Balance, but other athletes demonstrate the same principle. Squash may seem to be an "unbalanced" sport in that you play with just one hand. But you must get yourself balanced to hit the ball in the first place. And when you swing, you need to use your free hand to maintain your balance through the entire arc of the swing.

A good squash player, like a good tennis player, uses his free hand to balance himself for the shot. Take the racquet from his hand and he looks like a surfer balanced on a board riding the waves. The balanced stances in different sports are remarkably similar. The shortstop expecting a ground ball, the basketball player at the free-throw line, the batter at the plate, the golfer addressing the ball, the quarterback awaiting the snap—all have the expectant readiness for action that constitutes True Balance.

The martial arts may seem far removed from baseball, basketball, or golf. But in karate the participants start from the same athletic stance, the same balanced and ready position. Karate is not just a form of physical defense, but also a spiritual discipline. It is a holistic system that seeks to unify body, mind, and spirit. According to karate Sensei ("teacher") Taisen Deshimara, "Wisdom, intuition, and action are one." Wisdom pertains to spirit, intuition to mind, and action to body.

Karate is an ancient art, and references to early forms go back three thousand years. It developed at a time when an individual had to develop all capacities in order to survive and succeed. The individual had to achieve True Balance. So the discipline of karate, with its emphasis on developing the entire person—physical, mental, and spiritual—is still relevant today.

I wasn't surprised to learn that the physical practice of karate has three (the magical number!) categories. The triad of karate training consists of 1) *kihon* (stances, blocks, kicks, punches); 2) *kata* (sequences of traditional movement); and 3) *kumite* (actual sparring with an opponent). Furthermore, I learned that each *kata* has three aspects that correspond to my elements of True Balance. A *kata* trains the individual in 1) correct use of power (motion); 2) correct use of movement (rhythm); and 3) correct expansion and contraction of body (dimension).

Physical discipline—in sport, martial art, or dance—provides a vivid illustration of how True Balance operates and can be applied to all aspects of our lives. Balance is at the heart of each aspect—physical, mental, and spiritual. True Balance is the proper fusion and synthesis of all three. With True Balance, we are in a position to respond to whatever comes our way—finding the correct continuum of motion, calibrating the exact rhythm, and enlarging and perfecting the dimension of our action.

5

ACTING ON PURPOSE

Motion with purpose becomes true action. Purpose must be a conscious act of mind, born of rational decision and freedom of choice. Our unique conscience deliberates, and our reasoning brain chooses. Our highly developed conscience makes us responsible for all other living things. Our conscience and our consciousness give living a purpose beyond mere survival.

According to Latter-day Saint theology, as God's spiritually begotten children, we enjoy the gift of moral agency; that is, we are "agents unto [our]selves" (Moses 6:56). In the premortal world, Lucifer sought to revoke that sacred principle, and one-third of the hosts of heaven followed his misguided lead. The fact that we are here in mortality is evidence that we embraced the principle, which we also enjoy in this life. We are free to make decisions and choose the paths we will follow.

The catch is that we must also accept the consequences of our actions, and our choices are what determine our sorrows and joys. "The devil made me do it" is a common excuse, but it is a lie. We are what we have chosen to be, and our choices determine what we will be. In choosing, we become victims or victors.

Here is a diagram that illustrates how choice operates in the dynamic opposition of good and evil:

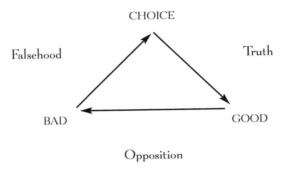

Figure 23– Illustration of Opposition

For freedom of choice to be meaningful, there must be opposition, and in this life there is opposition in all things. Religion teaches us that the most beneficial use of agency is to choose to do good and avoid evil. By doing so we realize our greatest potential and secure for ourselves the true happiness or joy that is the purpose of our existence.

True Action

To further emphasize the importance of human action, let's call beneficial human action "true action." History and experience demonstrate that human actions often do not rise above the instinctive actions of animals. Many shackle themselves through physical addictions and immoral behavior, thus surrendering their divine endowment of free choice.

True action, like True Balance, creates, builds, and grows. It doesn't resist or insist—it releases. It doesn't confine—it liberates. It doesn't destroy—it creates. But true action doesn't mean you have complete license to do whatever you please. Freedom without purpose or responsibility is like the Brownian Motion of random bouncing molecules.

True action, therefore, pursues a worthy goal. Set specific goals; beware of the deceptive fluctuations of aimless motion. Maintain your rhythm, pace yourself, and set intermediate and long-term goals. Setting intermediate and long-term goals is thinking three-dimensionally.

Pursuing a goal is essential to achieving True Balance. Consider the tightrope walker. According to Karl Wallenda, the great high-wire artist, the secret to keeping your balance while high up on the rope is to keep your mind and eyes focused on where you want to go. If you look down—or even look too closely at the rope under you—you lose your equilibrium and tumble to your destruction. For most of us, having a goal isn't an immediate life or death issue. But what you make of your life depends upon your balance, and achieving balance is impossible without having a goal.

Keep in mind the immediate and intermediate steps to your final goal. The high-wire walker sees his destination but continually shifts his focus to intermediate points as he moves forward. When I exercise on my treadmill, I need different focus points to keep my rhythm and motion in balance. If I just gaze around or stare at my feet, I find it difficult to stay on the moving machine. I must look at least one foot ahead to keep my balance. To advance toward your goal, keep looking to points ahead.

Everything in the universe is delicately balanced against gravity. As we move through our environment, gravity must stay in the center of our being to work *with* rather than *against* us. Walking is nothing more than achieving a helical rhythm that continually interrupts a fall. We catch ourselves with each step; instead of falling, we move forward—defeating gravity by staying in balanced motion.

Strive to make all your actions balance meaningfully. The three-dimensional manner in which we adjust to and thus overcome gravity teaches us how to meet and triumph over the inevitable obstacles of everyday life. Stay balanced and loose, roll with the punches, and move on.

Do the Thing

It's much better to be able to act than react. By taking action rather than passively reacting to events, we can make the moving world work for us, rather than the other way around. The golden rule is stated as an active principle, "Do unto others as you would have them do unto you." Notice that it isn't worded: "Be the kind of person you want others to be." That's also good advice, but not nearly as powerful as the command to *do*. Our true worth is revealed by our actions. Charity, the greatest of all virtues, is the active principle of faith and hope. Charity is love made manifest through action.

The American dream became a reality because from the beginning, action has been an American virtue. American philosophers such as Franklin, Thoreau, and Emerson are notoriously pragmatic. The emphasis on doing is particularly strong in Emerson's essays. "The law of nature is, do the thing and you shall have the power. That which we persist in doing becomes easier. Not that the nature of the task has changed, but our ability to do has increased." That thought has profoundly influenced my view of life.

Much of the time the task itself may not be difficult, but we make it difficult by not tackling it. The Stoic philosopher Seneca had this to say about taking action: "It is not because things are difficult that we do not dare; it is because we do not dare that they are difficult."

In our progressive triad of thinking, feeling, and doing, daring to do is the one thing we have the most control over. Feelings wash over us unbidden, and moods come and go. Thoughts can take hold of our mind in ways that seem beyond our control. Worry is wasted energy. The longer you carry a problem, the heavier it gets. I've found that just taking some kind of action can change my mood or sharpen my thinking. And the action doesn't have to be profound. Sometimes taking a walk, washing the car, getting a haircut, or just taking a bath can turn your mood around. Be optimistic, look for good, stay busy, and make it happen. Always stay happy with "an optimistic attitude expectant of good."

Laugh and Look for Humor

An essential ingredient of optimism is laughter. Of all his creations, God gave only human beings the gift of laughter. Mark Twain said that man was the only animal that laughed at himself, or needed to. We're really laughing at ourselves when we go to the zoo and laugh at the monkeys. It seems to me that monkeys are the funniest people. Or we could say that people are the funniest monkeys. When you are tempted to take yourself too seriously, think of the antics of the funny monkeys (after all, we are more like them than we think—we share about 99 percent of the same DNA).

A sense of humor requires a sense of the third dimension. To see the incongruity or absurdity of a situation, to laugh at yourself, learn to step outside of yourself. We need to occasionally adopt the attitude of Puck in A Midsummer Night's Dream who shook his head and muttered, "What fools these mortals be." So balance reality with humor. Laughter really is the best medicine, and it cures depression, loneliness, and boredom. "Laugh and the world laughs with you; weep, and you weep alone." No one has ever died from laughing.

Humor not only lifts your spirits, it can heal the body. When publisher Norman Cousins was diagnosed with a rare muscle disease, the doctors gave him the usual "six months to live." So Cousins set out to heal himself—with humor. He read comic novels and watched funny movies. The Marx Brothers films were his favorites, and he watched them over and over. He literally laughed himself back to health, adding years to his life, laughing until the end.

When you smile, you give yourself a "face-lift," and your mood lifts automatically. (Not only that, it takes only three muscles to smile, versus twenty-three to frown.) We are always warmed by the smile of another. In every way your own smile adds to your "face value."

A sense of humor prevents self-pity and helps keep the big picture in mind. I like a saying of the Lakota Sioux: "Sometimes I go about pitying myself. But all the while, I am being carried on the great winds across the sky."

Keep Dancing

I remember something that Rabbi Hillel, the great interpreter of Judaic law, wrote about the value of action and persistence: "I get up. I walk. I fall down. Meanwhile, I keep dancing." Dancing is a good metaphor for my idea of balance in rhythm and motion. Look at good dancers—solo, pairs, or ensemble. When they move to the music they are in balance, and to stay in balance they move to the rhythm, the beat, and the melody.

In our progressive triad of think, tell, do—thinking is primary, and how you think influences how you feel and determines the direction of your action. But inaction is the result of too little thinking—or maybe too much thinking. When I get into this state, I call it "analysis paralysis." If something needs to be done, just get on with it.

When you begin something, the motivation behind it is strengthened. Each time you act, every time you take a step, you reinforce your motivating principle. "For use almost can change the stamp of nature," said Shakespeare. In other words, "use," or practice, is more powerful than disposition or temperament.

A succession of good experiences expands optimism. You

develop an "attitude expectant of good." What you get is a "virtuous circle" that spirals upward and outward like an expanding helix. Those who get down on themselves and give up, end up in a vicious circle, squeezed like victims in a black hole, spiraling inward and downward.

The incremental increases pay off by a factor greater than the sum of each increment. Degree by degree water gets colder until it crystallizes into ice or warmer until it boils. In the same way, continual repetition of a good act moves you toward a new threshold. All you have to do is just take it one day at a time. You see it in sports, where tedious practice pays off by taking you to a new level of skill. Backhand after backhand may sail long or sink into the net, but if you stay with it, you'll eventually hit one down the line and win the match. Life is a process of persistent effort.

The Power of Repetition

Repetition in the pursuit of excellence changes the stamp of nature; it is the secret of success. "We are what we repeatedly do," said Aristotle. "Excellence is not an act, but a habit." Unfortunately, repetition in the wrong direction leads to bad habits, which become destructive addictions. Our bad habits are like beds—easy to get into, but hard to get out of.

The power of repetition is illustrated by Stephen Covey's story about the manager who was having a tough time organizing himself. Covey asked him if he could follow through on just one promise, which was to get up every day at 5:55 A.M. for just a week. He didn't ask the executive to chain himself to a rigorous minute-by-minute schedule or transform himself into a paragon of discipline. Covey simply asked him to get up at the same time each morning. Getting up at the same time was easy enough, as long as that's all he had to do.

But getting up earlier proved to be all he needed to do. Motivation to do more grew when he saw what he could accomplish by doing what seemed to be so little. Before long, the executive had disciplined himself and turned himself around. He had learned that a commitment to action had consequences far beyond the specific act. What a great lesson—the power of action alone can change your feelings, attitudes, and thoughts!

I'm an early riser, but I don't know if it came naturally. When I was a kid, Dad would have to pull me out of bed in the morning. I tried to avoid it whenever I could, but after a while I got used to it and made it part of my attitude to get a head start, not only on the day but also on the opportunities of life.

The power of action to change feelings, attitudes, and thoughts is shown in a story about Robert E. Lee. During the Civil War, Lee was torn by conflicting duties to nation and home. Jefferson Davis wanted Lee to lead the Confederate forces, but Lee kept vacillating. Finally Davis said, "Join first and then you'll feel committed." Action in such cases goes beyond setting the stage for commitment. Action can create meaning.

The power of action was also expressed memorably by Goethe: "Whatever you think you can do, or believe you can do, begin it." Actions always speak louder, and longer, than words, but unfortunately, not as often.

Great achievers act on the belief that they can indeed accomplish great things. They do things others say cannot be done. The achievers aren't necessarily more able than others; they are just more willing to view their mistakes as new opportunities. Achievers defy fear; achievers are focused, and (as you might expect) achievers are few. Emulators and imitators, on the other hand, are many. They may like to wear big hats, but they move no cattle.

True achievers care more about contributions than the superficial accoutrements of success. They travel light, speak softly, and wear their achievement easily. Their ultimate worth is what they give, not what they have.

Get Down to Business

When starting anything, it's easy to get stuck in the planning phase. Because of doubt or uncertainty, we fear taking that first step. The best way is to assume an attitude of "getting down to business." The power of action, in and of itself, is contained in the command of Jesus, "Seek and ye shall find; knock and it shall be opened unto you" (Matt. 7:7). It's a sad sight to see someone standing at the door but afraid to knock. The very act of knocking commits you to move forward through the door. There's danger in staring at the map but never venturing into new territory, afraid to seek out the treasures of life. The best hikes often happen when you blaze your own trail.

Here's another example of the power of action. Whenever he was asked to advise a company that was floundering, lacking direction, or mired in indecision, one of my management consultants would ask executives to write down ten "action points." The consultant didn't impart the latest management gimmick; he merely asked them to list and implement ten new things. Ten is not a magic number, though perhaps the clients were persuaded to follow the prescription by the subliminal association with the Ten Commandments.

"I've just found from experience," said the consultant, "that ten things seem to establish a kind of critical mass. I suppose seven or eight might also work, but I know for a fact that four or five are not enough. You need somewhere around ten to create sufficient attention to establish a new field of experience."

Move the Herd

In any activity, the idea is to keep moving. You hear sportscasters talking about momentum as if it were a mysterious protoplasm that ebbs and flows across the playing field. But momentum is real. Sustained motion increases the mass of any endeavor. Longfellow describes what happens when you slow down and stop: "On the plains of hesitation are the bleached bones of men who sat down to rest and resting, died."

At my White Sage Ranch, momentum is exemplified by the cowboys with their dogs as they transfer cattle from winter or summer range. They have to keep things moving. Sometimes they're ahead of the herd, sometimes behind, but they're always moving. Let's say they come to a dry watering hole. They don't get anywhere by sitting there and feeling sorry for themselves or blaming the universe for their bad luck. They must find another watering hole, or the herd will die. Or maybe they come to a swollen stream. They don't just turn back and hope things will be better tomorrow. They keep moving, until they find water shallow enough for the cattle to cross.

Energy is required to keep moving, but much more energy is required to keep stopping and starting. People who have a hard time starting something new keep looking back at previous projects. It's like a chess player who plays only one move at a time. It's hard to figure out your next move if you've concentrated all your energy on getting the knight to Q-5. When I play chess I try to look at least two or three moves ahead, searching for combinations that will lead to checkmate.

Here are two stories about the benefit of looking a few moves ahead. When I was a young guy, I used to wander around Salt Lake's east bench, telling curious onlookers I was looking for goat pasture. But it wasn't just pasture for goats. I was looking at lines of development and for land on which to build future homes. I was looking ahead to the probability that a viaduct over the mountains would be built to supply the area with water. Water was the missing third element in the basic triad that includes land and clean air. With the acquisition of water, the land, then only $25 an acre, would increase in value far beyond its ostensible worth as goat pasture.

My other story also involves water. It seemed to me that another reservoir could and would be built someday up around Hailstone Junction, the turn-off from Heber City to Francis and Kamas. So I began buying adjacent acreage on the mountain-sides very cheaply. Now Hailstone Junction lies at the bottom of the Jordanelle Reservoir. My land around the reservoir has three miles of lake frontage and has become valuable property for recreation and cabins. It's so valuable because it now has the three fundamental elements: good water, clean air, and scenic landscape.

Both stories illustrate how thinking three-dimensionally, searching for and finding the missing basic elements, gives you the opportunity to make the moving world work for you.

It's important to keep moving, but it's also important to know when to move on. Do something, then move on. Get on to the next thing, because the next thing is more important.

Figure 24– James L. Sorenson at White Sage Ranch 1999

Sometimes you must cut your losses. I like the lyrics of the song Kenny Rogers sings about the gambler, "You've got to know when to hold 'em, know when to fold 'em, know when to walk away, know when to run." The last line of the song imparts additional wisdom about focusing on what you're doing, rather than sitting back and enumerating your losses or gains. "You never count your money when you're sittin' at the table, there'll be time enough for countin' when the dealin's done."

One final thought about action while we're still using the metaphor of playing cards. It's something quite obvious, but it's a hard truth for many people. To win in the game of life you must sit down at the table. You can't just study the odds and lounge against the wall. You have to pull up a chair and say, "Deal me in."

6

DISCOVER YOUR PACE

As I have previously said, my dad exemplified the principle of pacing yourself. "Find your own rhythm and pace yourself," he said. He had discovered his own rhythm—measured, deliberate, and steady. He paced himself in everything, not just when he was hoisting a huge keg or digging a trench. My mother was more impatient and preferred a faster pace. She sometimes took risks to make things happen and disrupted her personal pace and rhythm. I became a blend of the dispositions of each parent—organized and work-oriented like my father, while acquiring some of my mother's risk-taking attitudes. I inherited my father's order, frugality, and deliberation and my mother's more social, self-sacrificing, and self-enterprising ways.

From my father's example I learned to be persistent. Dad never seemed to lose ground. Even when others were having trouble, he always seemed to be moving ahead, never stepping back—gaining ground inch-by-inch, step-by-step, slowly but surely.

I have a vivid memory of Dad's philosophy in action. As a little boy, I was walking to school one day past a job site where Dad was on a crew that was digging a trench. This was in the days before backhoes existed. Each man on the crew was paid for how many feet of trench he could dig in a day. Dad just

Emma Blaser Sorenson—   Joseph LeVoy Sorenson—
age 49   age 50
"Any virtue carried to an   *"Find your own personal*
excess becomes a vice."   *rhythm and pace yourself."*

Figure 25– My Parents in 1952

seemed to be plodding along, much slower than a big husky guy
farther down the road.

I walked over to my dad and pointed to the man, who was
digging much faster. "He's going to make a lot more money

than you today," I said in a worried voice. Dad just grinned. "Come back after school, son," he said.

Sure enough, when I showed up after school the big husky guy was barely lifting his shovel. He had disrupted his natural rhythm and worn himself out. Dad, on the other hand, was working at the same measured pace he had established earlier in the day, and he had dug at least a third more than the big guy.

Persistent, paced, and steady action will get most jobs done. But some jobs can be done at a fairly brisk pace. Many people dawdle simply because they don't have a clear idea of what it is they really want. They labor aimlessly and eventually grind to a halt.

Once you know what your goal really is, you advance with more energy and efficiency. That usually translates into a quicker pace. It's like the horse that sees the barn and gallops faster. We, too, work faster as we near the end of a project because the goal has become so clear. Finishing is exhilarating— the closer you get, the faster you go. Once a goal comes into sight, you feel a burst of energy that carries you across the finish line.

Samuel Johnson, the eighteenth-century essayist, critic, and teacher, advised his students to write their school compositions as fast as they could. He had found from his own experience that the faster he wrote, the harder he concentrated. But he also knew that at a certain point, meaning started to break down. A certain regularity of rhythm was required. He told his students to compose quickly but to gear back as their thinking out-raced their hand.

Of course, we shouldn't force our rhythm and make every piece of music allegro. Some things demand the walking pace of andante and others might require the slow measured pace of adagio. A steady pace seems to work for many things. Goethe said he worked "without haste, but without rest," keeping his pace slow but steady.

Moving without haste is finding your own rhythm, pacing yourself. Whatever your optimum natural rhythm, the main thing is to keep at it. Persistence has its own special reward. Nothing worthwhile is accomplished without persistence.

Perfectionism and Paralysis

Sometimes we don't complete things because of self-doubt and perfectionism. The danger of perfectionism is that we lose momentum and get bogged down in a quagmire of indecision. This becomes insidious because perfectionism then supplants the project. People actually start to take pride in their perfectionism, congratulating themselves on how exacting they are in their work. But having unreasonably high standards creates self-doubt and undermines self-esteem. A project never gets beyond being "a work in progress." Excellence, not perfection, must be our standard, at least in our mortal life. We should keep in mind that only Jesus lived the perfect life.

What would happen if John Stockton of the Utah Jazz expected every shot, every pass, every pick and roll to be perfect? He'd never let go of the ball or even make it to mid-court. In basketball, as in all sports, at some point you submit to the rhythm of the game and trust your skill and ability. Perfection eludes us all. The best shooters in the game miss more than half of their shots. Sometimes perfectionism leads to complete paralysis. As Coach Jerry Sloan puts it, "You miss 100 percent of the shots you don't take."

Bet on Yourself and Win

Many people slow themselves down by constantly questioning and doubting themselves. This is like trying to drive a car with one foot on the accelerator and one foot on the brake; it strains your engine, wastes your precious fuel of life, and prevents you from getting where you want to go. To advance toward any goal, we have to support and believe in ourselves at each step of the way. We can't organize our energies or achieve our goals unless we believe in ourselves and know we can succeed.

We do not need permission to think positively about ourselves. Too many of us wait for somebody to tell us we are capable, valuable, or lovable. All of us are guilty of this to some degree. When I had trouble speaking and learning to read in the first grade, the teachers labeled me "retarded." I was an adult before it was discovered that I have a condition called dyslexia, which made it difficult for me to interpret the shapes of letters and string them into words. My father must have been dyslexic as well, which would explain why he was always buying eyeglasses that never worked.

Overcoming what my teachers labeled retardation might be one of my greatest achievements. In so many instances, I had to look at things from a different angle two or three times to grasp and learn them. I believe my propensity to reason things out and think three-dimensionally comes from my dogged attempts to overcome dyslexia.

Stamp Your Own Visa

Don't look to others to define who you are. Your teachers tell you you're one thing, your parents, peers and employers may tell you that you're something else. But you are the one who has to determine the real truth about who you are. Letting others define you can cause much suffering. I learned many things from my dad, but one of the most important was to ignore the carping and criticism of others. I never saw a guy with so little inclination as he had to seek approval from others. I believe you don't need to worry too much about pleasing others as long as you believe in yourself and act in such a way that you feel good about yourself.

People consume vast amounts of energy and waste huge

amounts of time by waiting for someone to give them approval or permission to do what they want. Think of the movie *Casablanca* where everybody is sitting around waiting to get out of the city. But fortunately, we don't need exit visas to leave the wasteland of self-doubt and self-criticism.

To overcome excessive self-criticism, "be on your own side." You're the only person you're with every moment and in every situation. If you can learn to enjoy your own company, you overcome some of the worst scourges of life—boredom, loneliness, and rejection. So it's essential to be conscious of how you're relating to yourself.

Don't be your own worst enemy. Be your own best friend. Heal yourself with love. It pleases me to think that when you do so, it pleases your Creator because you're being kind to one of his greatest creations. When you treat yourself gently, you live closer to God, from whom all blessings flow.

What is the most important asset you own? Is it your house? Your car? Your stock portfolio? Your most important asset is none of these. It is you—everything else can be taken away. The best investment you can ever make is in yourself—your talents, your skills, your abilities.

The greatest success in life is finding and becoming your true self. Never stop growing. Your true wealth is the creative power of your own mind. Investing in the "Bank of You" brings big dividends. Put your time, money, and energy into the business of you.

Too often we seek fortune outside ourselves. True prosperity in life cannot come from the external world. It must evolve from within. Prosperity works from the inside out. Learn to nurture the god-within.

Love Yourself

Whenever you start to slide toward self-criticism, take an honest look at your life and keep looking until you find something positive about yourself. Start planting your own garden instead of waiting for someone else to bring you flowers.

Christ's commandment "Thou shalt love the Lord thy God with all thy heart, and with all thy soul, and with all thy mind" (Matt. 22:37) and his commandment "Thou shalt love thy neighbour as thyself" (Matt. 22:39) show us the way to inner peace and outer harmony. I believe much of the failure to follow Christ's injunction comes not from forgetting others, but from failure to love yourself. Love of self is necessary before we can love others; yet it is often overlooked and somehow assumed but not directly addressed—much less supported.

With the emphasis on loving God and your neighbor—loving others—some mistakenly think that such love is all-inclusive and doesn't include love of self. But to love God and love our neighbors, we also need to love ourselves. This consists of having a basic but humble respect for ourselves—a conviction that each of us is a child of God, and as such deserves to be recognized, heard, and appreciated. When we demean ourselves, we demean our Creator. After all, we are made in his image, and we should honor that image by loving ourselves, even as we love God and our fellow creatures.

Respecting and loving yourself has to do with knowing and understanding yourself. First, you face the truth about yourself. We all feel bad about the foolish things we've done. The important thing is to separate your behavior from who you are, so you can differentiate between who you are and what you've done.

Forget Failure

Though we must squarely face the truth of the wrong things we have done and resolve to act differently in the future, we must not lose our balance by looking backward and replaying hurts and heartaches and regrets over and over again. We should, of course, never forget what is worth remembering, but equally important, we should never remember what is best forgotten. Don't continue to play the same sad music. Forgive yourself and move on.

We form our identities in large part from our memories. If we brood on our failures, we define ourselves by those failures and keep them alive. People ask me about my failures, and I truly cannot remember them. Perhaps it's my unconscious survival system to forget losses. I basically remember my successes, and as a consequence, build on them and form my identity from them. Confidence and courage are fostered by memories of accomplishment.

Too many people keep failure alive by lamenting, "If only, if only, if only . . ." In doing so, they are like children who wake up from a bad dream but refuse to step out of their nightmare. The better way is to think, "Next time—next time I will. Next time—I can."

The phrase "next time" looks to the future. A powerful way to mobilize the future is to make a single three-letter word a permanent entry in your mental thesaurus. The word is *yet*. Faced with a daunting task, you can tell yourself, "I can't do it." Or you can say, "I can't do it, *yet*." Its use will transform a negative attitude into a positive one, lift you up when you are down, turn despair into hope. In his search for suitable filament for his light bulb, Thomas Edison embodied the "attitude of yet." As he experimented with one after another of thousands of materials, Edison never said, "I can't do it." Anyone passing through his laboratory in Menlo Park no doubt would have heard him mutter, "I can't do it, yet," or "it won't work, yet."

When you say, "I can't do it," you have failed. You're closing the door on possibility and opportunity. "I can't do it, yet" opens that same door. The "attitude of yet" encourages you to keep trying, working, and experimenting until you succeed. The little three-letter word is the operative definition of the success posture, "an optimistic attitude expectant of good."

Love in Three Dimensions

Many problems result from our failure to look at the complete three-dimensional nature of all things. We get stymied in the two-dimensional either/or, this or that, black or white, love yourself or your neighbor. If you're stuck in the two-dimensional trap, you think you have to follow one path or the other. You see only one or two possibilities. For instance, some individuals assume that they can love only their neighbor or only themselves. And since the emphasis falls on "love your neighbor," they foolishly think they must love only their neighbor, excluding concern for themselves.

The presiding principle of True Balance requires the crucial third dimension. In the injunction to love your neighbor as yourself, remember the key word *as*. In two-dimensional thinking, we allow the word *or* to replace the word *as*, creating the illusion that we have to choose one or the other. In reality, that little word *as* compels you to consider the crucial third dimension. It creates an additional category, which is not the same as loving only yourself, and not the same as loving only your neighbor, but loving your neighbor as, or in the same way as, yourself. This is the love that God has for each of us, a true example of balance in three dimensions.

The love you give yourself not only affects the love you give others but also affects the love you permit yourself to receive. If you're not "on your own side," it's much harder to believe others are on your side. Appreciate yourself, or you will not allow yourself to fully accept and receive appreciation from anyone else. How you relate to yourself determines how you experience God's love and the world relating to you. When you want a change, the way to begin is to notice how you are relating to yourself. Are you "on your own *case*," or are you "on your own *side*?" Being on your own case equates to being out of balance, creating self-inflicted wounds and imposing limitations on yourself.

When you are on your own case, you will be on others' cases; when you are on your own side, you will be on the side of others. In other words, we project our views of ourselves onto our brothers, sisters, and neighbors. In any encounter, how we see another person is a function of how we see ourselves. But a reciprocal process is also at work: we treat ourselves the way we treat others.

The ability to identify with self as we identify with others is at the heart of the Golden Rule, which is a profound prescription for spiritual growth. "Do unto others as you would have them do unto you" is ancient wisdom, a universal truth that is at the heart of all religions and ethical codes—Christianity, Judaism, Islam, Buddhism, Confucianism, Hinduism, Taoism, to name a few of the major belief systems. Give your fellowmen space in your personal kingdom, and you will have a place in theirs.

Criticism Is No Cure

If criticism cured things, the whole world would be healthy. But criticism, from yourself or from others, no matter how astute, rarely results in positive change. Instead of stimulating beneficial change, it usually spawns resentment and a defensive attitude. Even silly arguments with your husband or wife or other family members puts you on the defensive.

The first response to criticism is to put up a shield. It's like the instinctive response to a punch—we throw up our arms to deflect the blow. It really comes down to a deep instinct for survival. Your whole being reacts to protect itself. Even on a cellular level the reaction is protective. The cellular foot soldiers of the body's immune system rush in to ward off any foreign invasion.

Defensive energy is reactive and protective. Creative energy is proactive and venturing. Positive energy has neither time nor space for "can't, won't, don't." Eliminate the negatives. Look for

opportunities to say: "can, will do, yes, you bet, absolutely."
Make these important words a part of your everyday life:

> I apologize for my mistake.
> Let me make it right.
> Slay them with kindness and win with love.
> Run to daylight, look for the sun, and keep smiling.
> What else can I do for you?
> I'm glad you're here.
> Thank you.
> Yes.

How do you feel when someone has "gotten on your case," been negative, or critical of you? Chances are you find it difficult to sit back and philosophically consider the merits of the criticism. Under attack, you probably become dispirited and resentful. One of the great ironies of self-criticism is that it invites criticism from others. At the heart of most human problems is the lack of self-respect and self-esteem. We often sell ourselves too short, too soon, and too cheaply. We can accomplish complex and intricate tasks only when we persevere and believe in ourselves.

When we believe in ourselves we will believe in others. I tell my children and grandchildren to act gently and non-violently toward others. Slay them with kindness and win them with love. That's the way. When we believe in each other and act out of mutual esteem, cooperation is possible and we deal more creatively and productively with each other. When our actions stem from love, they result in peace.

Searching for our spiritual roots and identity, we become one with the emerging world family, for as John Donne reminded us, no man is an island, no one stands alone. We are all interconnected. Our commonality is revealed in the double helix of our DNA and enacted in our shared cycle of life. We may seem as dissimilar as scrub oaks and giant sequoias, but we're all essentially alike. We have a common source. We are the branches and leaves on the great tree of life, all of us rooted in the image and likeness of God.

The superficial differences of color, creed, or conflicting tribes can truly separate us. But tolerance, goodwill, and love go a long way toward reconciling these differences. Each of us is different and that difference makes each of us one-of-a-kind—unique, important, and special. We should celebrate that uniqueness for what it is—something wonderful, glorious, and magnificent. This celebration is another expression of oneness and love.

III
RHYTHM

7

MOVE TO
NATURE'S RHYTHM

∽০∾

Our environment is marked by the rhythm and measured by the cycle of many natural forces: seasons, tides, day and night, and we are conditioned by and respond to the richly varied rhythms of nature about us. The earth itself "breathes," its atmosphere being balanced by the rhythmic exchange of free oxygen and carbon dioxide. Our internal systems are patterned and balanced by our biological rhythms—the systole and diastole of our beating hearts, inhaling and exhaling the breath of life, the cycle of sleeping and waking.

Scientists continue to discover much about our biorhythms—or circadian rhythms—and how they precisely recalibrate and balance all our physiological systems. From the chemistry of our cells to the cycles of our sleep, the circadian rhythms control body temperature, heart rate, and the secretion of such things as sweat, melatonin, cortisol, and growth hormone.

We achieve our individual best when our personal rhythms are in sync with the rhythms of the natural world. There was a time when our work and play were tied to the changing seasons and the rising and setting sun. People used to tell time by the change of seasons and the progress of the sun across the sky. Time was for them, therefore, as much a dimension of the world as the landscape in which they lived. Planting and harvest took place in concert with the pulsating rhythms of nature.

Today our lives are ruled by the man-made clock instead of the rhythms of nature. We manipulate time into artificial shapes rather than participate in its natural flow. We are conditioned to seek instant stimulation and gratification wherever possible, and we foolishly bloat ourselves with fast foods and then starve ourselves with quick weight-loss diets.

The natural flow of time is a dimension of God's time, which in reality springs eternally from his mind and is truly "timeless." When we take arbitrary divisions as absolute reality, we attempt to impose our man-made time onto God's time. It is a failure of imagination to try too literally to reconcile scientific and spiritual duration. When the Bible tells us that God created the world in six days, and rested on the seventh, we should not assume that God's day is the same as our own. What is instructive in the Genesis account of the Creation is the pattern that is revealed: six days of labor followed by a day of rest. True Balance recognizes a life cycle that involves a rhythm of activity and rest, that we cycle in and out of periods, eras, and ages. We cycle in and out of time, but God inhabits the dimension that defines time.

We should adopt nature's rhythms of activity and rest. Our internal clock, with its exquisitely sensitive balance wheel, requires time and attention to recalibrate itself. The truth is, when we attempt to "squeeze" time, the more life we lose and the less we achieve. My Great-Grandfather Hans Olaus Sorenson once revealed to me the secret of his long, long life: "I work hard, and take a short nap every day."

As a youngster, I had such abundant energy that I didn't heed Great-Grandfather Sorenson's advice about naps. But as the clock keeps ticking and I move a little more slowly, energy diminishes and therefore becomes more precious. I take a nap in the afternoon and use the restful interlude to contemplate what I've done during the day and what I will yet do.

When you tune in to the rhythms of work and play, activity and rest, you accomplish much more. Instead of fighting time, you're flowing with it and making it work for you.

Today everything is Bang—Zip—Pow! We're assaulted by excitement for excitement's sake. Nothing is as boring, irritating, and wearing as constant noise and incessant stimulation. Natural excitement, when it occurs within the everyday rhythm of relaxation and activity, is healthy. Instead of depleting body and spirit, it nurtures and renews them. True excitement is recreation in the truest sense: it re-creates us physically, emotionally, and spiritually.

Again, balance is the key. Modern technology has given us ever-increasing speed, but hasn't increased our ability to manage it. When we lose our natural rhythm, we become disoriented, and we eventually self-destruct. When we find our own rhythm and pace, we are empowered to work with our environment, meet our goals, and become masters of our fate.

The Nature of Rhythm

Every living thing is in motion. True Balance is motion modulated by rhythm, and our journey through life is a pageant of rhythmic motion. We crawl, we walk, we run. It's fascinating to watch babies crawl. They demonstrate an inborn sense of rhythm as they synchronize left hand with right leg and vice versa. This rhythmic motion gives them the needed balance to scoot along the carpet. This "cross-patterned" motion of our limbs is the basis of our body's internal balance system and continues to develop as we learn to walk, skip, and run.

More and more, doctors and medical researchers are recognizing the body's need for active movement and finding unexpected benefits in everyday exercise. Dr. Andrew Weil, for one, says ordinary walking does more than burn calories and get your heart pumping. He recommends walking precisely because of the cross-patterned rhythm it provides. When you walk, the right leg and the left arm move forward simultaneously; then the left leg and the right arm repeat the pattern. According to Dr. Weil, this motion generates electrical activity in the brain that harmonizes the entire central nervous system. Physical motion and rhythm thus enhance intellectual and spiritual balance.

Take a Walk

I've felt that harmonizing influence when I take walks. The steady rhythmic motion balances both body and spirit. When you are stymied by some problem, I recommend that you take a walk. It will help rebalance you physically, mentally, and spiritually.

Go outside and listen for the wind and surprise yourself by actually hearing it. I've been out when at first I couldn't hear anything; but when I listened more carefully, I could hear the birds singing above and all around. But you don't have to go for a walk in the woods. Take a walk in the city. You'll see a lot of people who move more like robots than robust human beings. They clutch their problems to their chests instead of swinging their arms and striding forward with a lively expectation that something good is going to happen.

Often in the morning, I hop onto my treadmill, swinging my arms and legs to get into a good walking rhythm. After five to ten minutes I have restored my physical balance. My heart is pumping and my blood is flowing, giving me added mental energy to tackle and solve today's problems. When I'm physically balanced and mentally sharp, I'm more equipped to find all those crucial third dimensions.

Personal rhythm means going with the flow on the freeway of life. When your own rhythm is in balance, you're better able to synchronize with your fellow drivers, getting a feel for the road and responding to unpredictable stops and starts. Instead of fighting traffic, you flow with it. Force things and you will find yourself sideswiped or rear-ended. Establishing your personal rhythm and moving at your own pace create a safer, smoother path to your destination.

Find Your Rhythm

Discover your own personal rhythm for work. You may prefer to handle only one thing at a time. I like to have several things going on at once—my entrepreneurial and innovative enterprises require that I move from one thing to another—closing a real estate deal, developing video technology, innovating medical devices, working on a cure for bladder cancer, devising new tools for DNA sequencing. I pace myself to keep my interactions with people efficient as I manage, perfect, and grow an enterprise. For me, a change in focus is as refreshing as an energizing rest.

I remember Dad telling me that pacing yourself and finding your personal rhythm was the secret to success. Find your rhythm and then live within it. Dad said, "Pace yourself and be your own man." Since he did so much physical work, pacing himself properly was essential to staying with it and persisting in getting things done. But pacing yourself and finding the right rhythm doesn't apply only to physical prowess. It's even more important when using the part of the body that's found above the neck. You must find the right intellectual rhythm and pace yourself accordingly.

As far as my own mental pace goes, I like private conferences, but it doesn't bother me to have several people in my office at the same time. I try to eliminate unnecessary entrances and exits, gearing up and down for each meeting. Sharing ideas and knowledge in one meeting rather than three or four creates team spirit. Doing things sequentially, one after another, is often more tiring and time-consuming than doing them simultaneously. Doing things together can be energizing; I call it "TEEM" (time, energy, motion) work.

I maintain my rhythm by planning a new endeavor before finishing a current project. Many people work to be able to say, "I have arrived, I am there now." But that's a deceptive, smug, and static way of looking at the world. Life is a process of continual change—by minutes, days, and years. If you don't continually set new, meaningful goals, you will expire from inertia. Since we are what we have been, and since we are fast becoming what we will be, the need to set worthwhile goals and move steadily toward them is paramount.

I keep moving on to new things. I never thought when I started selling pharmaceuticals in 1946 that some day I would be innovating and manufacturing some of the fastest and most advanced DNA sequencing methods. Back in the 1950s, scientists Crick and Watson were trying to figure out just what DNA was. Now with the latest DNA sequencing methods, I'm involved in an exciting never-before-dreamed-of science. We are now looking at, learning about, and understanding the very essence of life.

When I sold pharmaceuticals in the 1940s and 1950s, making a long-distance phone call was still a technological wonder. Now, in the new millennium, I'm innovating precise and selective image compression for real-time tele-conferencing. The new technology keeps me excited about living, and the work keeps me looking at the global picture to foster heart-to-heart understanding around the world.

No matter how involved I am in my work, I strive to keep balanced by being available to my kids and grandkids, even during working hours. Their calls are welcome interruptions and always give me a lift. I enjoy hearing about their everyday activities, their special occasions, and their hard-won achievements. Being part of their lives keeps me young.

Make Every Move Count

I said earlier that dancing is a good metaphor for balance in motion and that good dancers, whether they dance alone, with a partner, or with a troupe, must stay in balance. To do so, they move in precise rhythm. Precise motion is nothing more than making every move count, just the way my dad did when he was chopping wood or stacking kegs or digging a trench. Hoisting those beer kegs three-high required precise rhythm. Because he moved with True Balance, he could often do the work of two ordinary men.

The right rhythm makes every move count and makes everything look easy. Observe Fred Astaire, a master of his art. When dancing he never seemed to sweat. But he worked meticulously to get every move just right. Because he learned so well what he had to do, he could move with seeming spontaneity and effortless grace.

Even in a start and stop game like squash, you need to find your rhythm. As you play a point, the rhythm and beat of the bouncing ball paces your moves on the court. In soccer, action is continuous, but it ebbs and flows, and players pace themselves to stay in the rhythm of the game. In baseball, a successful hitter learns the rhythm of the opposing pitcher—fast or slow, smooth or herky-jerky—and times his swing to pick up the ball as it leaves the pitcher's hand.

Play to Stay in Rhythm

When you get a feel for physical rhythm, you understand why athletes are forever talking about it. Michael Jordan had this to say about his feel for the game: "I don't know if I can ever explain this to people who don't play basketball. There's a certain rhythm you play at and somehow that rhythm can be distorted for various reasons. You have to play to stay in rhythm, whether it's in practice or in a game." I especially like that last sentence: "You have to play to stay in rhythm." That's just another way of saying how important it is to keep moving, to keep doing, and to keep going. It's honoring your own rhythm and pacing yourself.

John Stockton talks about how important it is to get the right rhythm when performing the "pick and roll" with Karl Malone. With his cerebral approach to the game, Stockton is a great example of how "court sense" can count for more than size and speed. You often see players running up and down the court with little rhythm or purpose. Stockton somehow manages the pace of the game, varying his speed according to defensive alignment and intuitively waiting until just the right moment to throw a pinpoint pass to a teammate. He knows when to gamble and when to play it safe.

Rhythm might be a mysterious matter for those who haven't played sports or done much physical work. Rhythm has to do with efficiency and making moves in the most elegant ways. As different as Dad was from Fred Astaire or Michael Jordan, he was every bit their equal in the elegance of his motion. Instead of making many unnecessary, strained movements, he made every movement count. Like a master artist, he had developed an economy of means, and there was beauty in his approach to work.

Know What You Want to Catch

You can only move with your personal rhythm if you know exactly what you want to accomplish. When you set a goal, you move with purpose. If you don't have a goal, you'll wander helplessly or increase your speed to make up for your lack of direction. There's no beauty in aimless wandering. It's like freeform dancing, lurching this way and that. There is no art and it certainly isn't beautiful to watch. The dancer soon becomes bored and tired. Energy and beauty are born of a graceful pattern of movement.

Our life was not meant for aimless motion. To win in the

game of life, be explicit about tasks, targets, and goals. Focus on your goals, and aim for your target. If you're fishing for trout, take fly-casting equipment, but if you want bass, you'd better bring along sinkers and live bait.

Achievers are goal-seeking people. They begin each task with a goal in mind, then find a way to achieve it, whether it is fishing for trout, creating a business, or living a life.

The Rhythm of Happiness

Happiness, like life, is something in motion and manifests its presence in a regular rhythm. It manifests itself, because it won't come if you chase it. Happiness arrives when you aren't looking for it. It is a by-product of a balanced life—when love, family, friendship, work, and play are blended in a harmonious whole.

Happy people fix their minds on some object other than their own happiness. They seek the happiness of others, the improvement of humankind, or excellence in work. Aiming at something else, they find happiness by the way. Many bring happiness *wherever* they go; others, however, create happiness only *whenever* they *leave*.

Some have the notion that happiness is an extreme state, a scream of bliss. This leads them to seek happiness in extreme, transitory, emotional experiences. They court physical danger to get their adrenaline pumping. The excitement may be real, but it's always momentary. To replicate the experience, they raise the stakes, and end up gambling with their lives. This happens with tobacco, alcohol, and illicit drugs—more is needed each time to satisfy the addiction and to produce a "high."

The highs found in courting danger and taking drugs are inevitably followed by extreme lows. Because the human organism seeks balance in all things, nothing that happens to us is one-sided. In fact, excruciating lows might go deeper and last longer than euphoric highs, as a stressed system attempts to reset, recalibrate, and balance. Thus the saying: "The higher the tide, the stronger the undertow."

Instead of illicit drug-induced emotional roller coasters, True Balance creates serene natural horizons—the rhythms of life vibrating to the complete range of natural human experience. Joy comes not from extreme experience, but from modulation, measure, and moderation; it isn't the jagged flash of lightning, but the glow of the sky at sunrise. I learned about the danger of extremes from my mother. She was forever reminding me that "any virtue carried to an excess becomes a vice."

Today our new imbalances are the mirror images of the old; they are poverties of excess, not needs. We have no lack of food. Obesity is frequently a disease of the poor, who often lack an understanding of good nutrition. Outlandish music and television have created a new poverty of imagination; only the rich in mind read books. Safety used to be scarce; now we pay extra for risk and the illusion of danger. We prize status in material goods, not because we can have them but because others don't. We have not learned the perennial lesson that true wealth is a life filled with meaning, joy, and love.

Still, there are richer and poorer all about us. Poverty has endured, but not because we lack material resources; our poverty is in our distribution, not our supply. Our abundance fuels ever more wretched excess, and conspicuous consumption becomes the highest good. The lessons taught by the man from Galilee still hold: the kingdom of heaven is attained not by amassing the riches of the world, but by acting with a humble, grateful, and charitable heart.

Another imbalance is in the modern relationship between men and women. In different times and different cultures, a variety of arrangements and patterns of interaction between men and women have existed. In our own age we've witnessed a needed correction in the "balance of power" between the sexes. Women have asserted themselves in a full range of cultural institutions—politics, business, religion. I'm happy that my daughters and granddaughters have more options open to them than women of previous generations.

Nevertheless, I think it must be tough to be a young man these days. A few elements of our culture have exploited the issue of gender equity and are openly hostile toward traditional masculinity. The natural rough and tumble of small boys is seen as dangerously aggressive. Ideologues who argue that differing male and female characteristics are cultural artifacts ignore inherent biological inclinations. If you pay close attention to the behavior of children, you will notice that boys and girls are genetically "wired" to behave in different ways.

One university study put small children into a room with a doll house and left them alone to see how they would play with it. The girls proceeded to set the dolls to work in conventional homemaking tasks. The boys, on the other hand, put the doll figures on the roof, and had them slug it out and tumble to the ground below.

It's important for boys and girls to have equal opportunities, but I hope the push for equality doesn't somehow subvert the natural tendencies of girls and boys to be different. I regret that young men today have lost cultural certainties that guided men of earlier generations. Too many boys don't have a father in their home and are therefore deprived of an immediate and ongoing example of what it means to be a responsible man. In today's distorted environment, many men fail to develop traditional masculine qualities of assertiveness, ambition, and accountability.

The "anything goes" attitude about private behavior also needs to be challenged. Looking at the big picture, we know that our inborn and God-given biological dispositions will endure. But so delicate are the transactions between nature and nurture that in specific instances desires and dispositions can be tilted out of balance. In such an environment, the precarious identity of an adolescent can be devastated.

Consider, for example, how a lot of young people look at marriage these days. I read one study that found that many teenagers see nothing wrong with having kids outside of marriage.

Despite such alarming trends, I'm confident the pendulum will swing back to embrace traditional values. Nature constantly seeks to balance itself. Looking at the big picture again, we know that these trends will shift. Already there is a growing movement among teenagers to pledge chastity before marriage. I see a powerful life rhythm working to reassert the True Balance of the family.

Parental example is by far the most powerful way to instruct children, and it is in a loving family that a child can best learn how to exercise moral agency and choose the right path in life. Cultural fashions and amoral license must not supplant family values and eternal verities.

The Rhythm of Thought

Thinking is structured by the rhythm of dialogue. We talk to ourselves in our head. Remember the last time you surprised yourself by speaking out loud the very words you had been mulling over in your mind. We pose questions to ourselves and then answer them. Interior monologue quickly becomes dialogue.

A dialogue is not necessarily a two-dimensional exchange. Conversation between two people always creates an unspoken third dimension. That dimension is the shared reality of the talkers and could be the weather, sports, travel, movies, religion, or culture. Notice how often when we meet someone for the first time, we somehow find common ground in a mutual friend or acquaintance, school, or work.

Dialogue really means the "way of discussion," and the best dialogues involve more than just two participants; you need at least three to establish the full dimension of a serious discussion.

When I think of the kind of dialogue that goes on inside our minds, I picture those cartoons where a character is trying to make up his mind and finds himself caught between his "good angel" and "bad angel." But the debate doesn't have to be of a moral nature. Anytime we think, different voices pipe up in our heads. These voices represent conflicting parts of ourselves or alternative courses of action. Our interior voices also speak the various roles we all play in everyday life—parent, husband, wife, employee, son, daughter, friend, neighbor. Much of our thinking, in fact, consists of trying to balance the duties and responsibilities of our various roles.

Your most productive thinking flows not necessarily easily, but progressively, persistently, and purposefully. That flow comes from the dynamic rhythm of interior discussion, where all options are considered and everything is weighed in the balance. You can't think logically if one voice is shouting louder than all the others.

The same principle applies in ordinary conversation. The best speakers neither shout nor whisper, but modulate and vary their voices. They use rhythm, intonation, and emphasis to win and retain the listener's attention. The words of a good speaker caress your ears and stimulate your own thinking.

Classical authors were versed in the art of elocution and knew the power of the spoken word. Plato wrote his philosophy in a series of dialogues, with various characters presenting different viewpoints. The give and take of dialogue was a realistic way to present his ideas. But the give and take of debate also models the actual activity of the mind. We all mentally rehearse arguments with friends and family, imagining what they will say and how we will answer.

We don't automatically think in well-organized paragraphs, neatly subdivided into logical categories. Thinking is a process of discovery and rediscovery that moves to the rhythm of thesis, antithesis, and final synthesis.

Notice that we find ourselves looking again at a three-part structure. An original idea evokes a counter-idea, and the debate reshapes them into the new synthesis of a third idea.

We often get stuck in extreme positions when we debate. This is the dualistic thinking I warned about earlier. Instead of looking for the third dimension, either in a synthesis of the conflicting ideas or in an alternative solution, we just hold on tighter to our original ideas. We dig in and soon find ourselves in so deep that we can't climb out. We should always explore the surrounding terrain for higher ground and look for the third dimension.

All too often, public discussion—especially of ideas people care about—turns into acrimonious debate. This is a distortion of the natural rhythm of thought and produces nothing of value. What should be an orderly discussion becomes an antagonistic argument. When everything is black or white, other shades are ignored. When everything is "thumbs up" or "thumbs down," you lose the benefit of sideways, forward, backward, and in-between.

The media encourage dualistic, two-dimensional, yes-or-no thinking. Important issues are framed in simplistic for-or-against terms, and people on two sides of an issue trot out to mouth their ten-second sound bites. Even the so-called "serious" programs like CBS's *Sunday Morning* or NBC's *Nightline,* or the *News Hour* on PBS are structured like debates. They're complete with "experts" propped up like Punch and Judy puppets, each taking a whack at the other, after which the moderator materializes on camera to thank everyone for coming and to say, "We'll see you all next time." Nothing's been resolved, no idea has been developed, and no discussion has deepened our understanding.

Artificial debates have an exaggerated rhythm. They remind me of a teeter-totter with angry elephants. There's never any chance of achieving balance because the elephants keep crashing up and down. Achieving balance requires a careful calibration of the weight of one idea against another. Such calibration encourages us to synthesize polarized opinions and form a third perspective. According to common wisdom, there are two sides to every story; I recommend that you go beyond the common and look for the third side.

The Rhythm of Learning

My first lesson about the rhythm of learning was accidental. I was having a hard time learning how to read. My teachers tried to get me to concentrate by making me sit still as a stone and stare hard at the book. But the letters transposed themselves, and the words danced on the page, refusing to assemble themselves into meaningful sentences.

I discovered by chance that reading came easier when I was sitting by myself in my little red rocking chair, where I felt secure and safe, comforted by the gentle to and fro motion of the chair. The rhythmic rocking imparted a rhythmic pattern to the words on the page. "The *little* dog *fetched* the *stick*." The measured motion allayed the anxiety that otherwise rendered me mentally immobile. Rhythm helped me master the unfamiliar words and make sense of them.

I thought of my little rocking chair when I was in Jerusalem a few years ago and watched people praying at the Wailing Wall. I noticed they were rocking back and forth as they chanted their prayers. I learned that the Standing Prayer, or Amidah, involves a ritual bowing at regular intervals. The ritual bowing is a three-part procedure: bend knees, bend forward while straightening the knees, then return to a standing posture.

My rhythmic rocking and the Jews' rhythmic bowing are certainly different. But both demonstrate the principle of rhythm and show how body and mind are interdependent. In each case, rhythmic, physical motion produces intellectual and emotional balance, which in turn create the serenity that facilitates both prayer and learning.

I have since discovered that I am part of the 5% of the population affected by dyslexia or "word blindness." Brain scientists theorize that dyslexia arises in the auditory cortex, which serves as a gateway for sounds. Dyslexic persons are less able to process the stream of rapidly changing sounds—phonemes—that constitute spoken language. Dyslexic persons also have a hard time learning to read because they don't immediately connect words on the page with words they hear. My rhythmic "rocking solution" allowed me to separate the phonemes and thus connect the shapes on the page with the spoken word. With my own rhythm and pace, the words finally began to make sense.

The lesson I learned about rhythm and learning wasn't something I was conscious of at the time. Only in looking back on the experience do I see how I happened on to the rhythm of learning—we employ the natural and familiar to master something new.

Overcoming Fear of the Unknown

All learning is structured by a dynamic rhythm: we move from the known to the unknown. This two-part dialectic may seem to contradict my concept that everything has at least three dimensions. What's the missing dimension, then? It's the transformation of the unknown to something known, but more important, it's reshaping or adding dimension to what you already know. This is what assimilation and correlation are all about. When you learn something new, you assimilate information and correlate it with what you already know. In the process, the shape of what you already know gains added texture, depth, and dimension.

People who fear the unknown magnify their ignorance by imagining something menacing and threatening. It reminds me of old maps where unexplored territories were marked with the warning, "Here be monsters." Today we know what's on the other side of the map, so we worry about what's out there in space. Instead of threatening serpents over the horizon, the fearful imagination invents space aliens that appear in the night and abduct people from their beds.

Fear of the unknown also operates in ways that are not so obviously primitive. People can get very clever in rationalizing their behavior. They crouch in fear and cling to what they know rather than stride into the unknown. Many people, for instance, are afraid of the computer. It seems intimidating, unfamiliar, cold, and anti-human. Once you get the hang of it, however, the computer is not just an efficient tool, it's a friendly instrument that has become vital in human communication. That's why I've embraced personal computing and am developing a new teleconferencing system using personal computers, TV, and interactive video with telephony.

Fear of the unknown sometimes stops people just when they are on the verge of a great breakthrough. Fear whispers in their ears, "Well, here we are safe, that's enough." Comfortable with what they have and fearful they'll lose it if they look for more, they're afraid to create something new or look for a better way.

The prevailing sentiment of a lot of folks is to "stick with what you know." Imagine where that philosophy would have gotten us in the field of medicine. We'd still be trying to cure sick people with magical potions and mystical chants. It was a giant step into the unknown to cut open and look inside the human body. For most of human history, the actual workings of the human organism were a mystery. It wasn't until 1628 that William Harvey proved that blood is always in motion, circulating through the body to the rhythm of the beating heart.

The rhythm of learning, moving from the known to the unknown, is consistent with the triangle of perception I noted earlier—*learning, knowing,* and *understanding.* When you learn, you take in new information, but you don't really get to the third level until you can connect it up with what you already know.

Sandwiches and Symphonies

Creative work requires finding True Balance through your own personal rhythm. It doesn't matter whether you're composing a symphony, making a scientific discovery, or assembling a submarine sandwich—the work must proceed with the proper rhythm. If not, you end up with a lot of noise, or lettuce and salami all over the place. You can learn a lot about rhythm by watching a skilled sandwich maker. In fact, you can probably learn more about rhythm by watching a sandwich maker than you could if somehow you eavesdropped on the creative process of a composer or scientist. That's because the sandwich maker does his creative work out in the open. The sandwich is assembled before your very eyes. Slicing bread, stacking meat and cheese, spreading condiments, and adding lettuce are all accomplished to the beat of a perceivable rhythm.

Composers, painters, and poets give similar accounts of how they create. Common to all is the concept of rhythm. They describe alternating periods of work and rest, of intense activity followed by seeming passivity. But the passive stage isn't really all that inactive. Much is going on under the surface. It's like a duck on a pond that appears to be just gliding along but is really paddling hard under the surface.

This is similar to the kind of assimilation that takes place in learning. The mind is always in motion, whether you realize it or not. Dreaming, a kind of assimilation, is evidence of this. The mind is sorting out the scattered impressions of the previous day, constructing narratives from the bits and pieces of present reality and past memory. Art forms are a more ordered example of this process, with rhythm acting as the organizing principle. Rhythm forms art from the sights, sounds, and feelings of past experience. Rhythm also disciplines and orders our desires, dreams, and fantasies into three-dimensional, meaningful artistic structures.

The rhythm of intense concentration and relaxed reverie, of precise focus and free reflection, is typical of all creative work. Examples abound of how scientific discoveries fit this model. After a long day of conscious and disciplined thinking about the atomic structure of the benzene molecule, August Kekule "slept on the problem" and dreamed of atoms dancing in a chain. His unconscious mind had assimilated information and formed it into an elegant theory.

Concentration and Unconscious Creation

You might suppose that mathematics is totally conscious and logical and that the rhythm of unconscious assimilation plays no part in mathematical thinking. But the testimony of great mathematicians proves otherwise. The French mathematician and physicist, Jules Henri Poincaré, revealed how important a period of unconscious "work" is to solving mathematical problems. Poincaré describes how the cycle of intense concentration and relaxed reverie works: "Often when one ponders a hard question, nothing is accomplished with the first attack. Then one takes a rest, long or short, and sits down to work again. During the first half-hour, as before, nothing is found, but then all of a sudden the crucial idea pops into the mind."

Poincaré gives this example of how a crucial idea about quadratic equations came to him following the rhythm of hard work and relaxation: "Disgusted with my failure to solve the problem, I went to spend a few days at the seaside and thought of something else. One morning, walking on the bluff, the solution suddenly came to me, with complete clarity and certainty."

What I find interesting in his explanation is how he was relaxing. He was taking a walk. In my father's phrase, Poincaré "found his own rhythm and paced himself." I'm inclined to think that the rhythm of a seaside stroll and fresh air helped inspire the mathematical solution. You get a lot more energizing oxygen to your brain if you're walking outside instead of sitting in a cramped office.

Writing of any sort requires creative thinking. Gestation follows initial conception. You need to give your subconscious time to play around with ideas and sort them into new combinations. I remember reading about how Charles Dickens would spend hours and hours walking around London late at night, staying away from his writing table until he felt that his stories were ready to leap from his pen onto the page.

Dickens did his best thinking while he was out walking. Walking helped improve breathing and circulation to the brain, enriching his creative power. Remember what Dr. Weil said about the harmonizing rhythm of walking? The cross-patterned rhythm of the right leg striding to the swing of the left arm generates electrical activity that harmonizes the central nervous system. And what is harmony but balance? Walking through the night streets of London, Dickens was calling upon all dimensions of his physical and spiritual life to create his novelistic world.

Finding the right rhythm is crucial for creating anything— whether it's a symphony or a sandwich, a poem or a pie. But rhythm also allows you to work on several creations or projects concurrently. If you pace yourself, you can move from project to project and draw energy from changing the focus of your work. As in everything, the secret is balance and distributing your attention in such a way that your energy is renewed, rather than dissipated. Establish your own personal rhythm so you feel and know when to stop what you're doing and move on to something else.

Some people need to work on one thing at a time. They need to finish a project and resolve the creative tension before focusing on something else. Others thrive on working on several things at once. I don't mean you should do things simultaneously—like people on the freeway who are chatting on their cell phones, eating bagels, combing their hair, and reading the paper while trying to maneuver though traffic. I'm talking about people who can give their total attention to one thing, then another, and still others in turn. Each project proceeds to completion concurrently with the others. Turning from one project to another can often generate energy instead of depleting it. A change can build a reservoir of energy fed by the flow of various projects. The more I do, the more energy I generate; the more energy I generate, the more I want to do and the more I am able to do.

The Stages of Creation

Creativity breathes to the rhythm of focused thought and relaxed reverie, of discipline and dream. Creativity demands a maturity of thought that comes from persistent curiosity and hard thinking. Without conscious effort, dreaming produces little. With your eyes wide open, look around and "find a better way" to create your unique vision.

The rhythm of creation, like everything else in our three-dimensional world, is structured by the principle of three. Every creative act has three stages: germination, assimilation, and completion. The first and third stages are active, while assimilation, the second stage, though quiet and seemingly passive, represents activity in a non-conscious mode.

The rhythmic cycle of creation simulates the birth cycle. Germination is the same as conception, where the whole process is initiated in a burst of energy. Assimilation has its equivalent in gestation, the stage when the fetus grows and develops. Completion is analogous to giving birth; your creation is now separate and independent.

Germination

Germination involves a great deal of kinetic energy. Any beginning is buzzing with energy—you are optimistic, confident, and hopeful. You have big dreams and visions of success. At the beginning of any project—a business, a party, a trip, a job, or a diet—everything is potential and possibility. You're setting the stage, and the stage can be as big as the world.

Because the energy is so high during germination, many people spend their lives at this stage. They make plans, fantasize, and scurry about in preparation. They're forever "resetting the stage," running this way and that, switching scenery, preparing, rearranging, replacing props and partners. They don't move forward to where they can shop their options and shed the excess. They don't reach the crucial point of action or carrying through. Always start the germinating stage by focusing on a specific goal or course of action. This lays the groundwork for assimilation.

Assimilation

Assimilation, like gestation, is an internal process. Your new creation is growing and developing according to its own rhythm. Assimilation is the most subjective stage of creation because you're drawing on all your inner resources. Everything you've learned and all the consequences of your choices now come into play. Without consciously deliberating, your mind now creates new connections among various parts of your knowledge, and new perceptions are formed.

The mind's ability to find new connections is one definition of creativity. Kids are creative because everything is new to them and their brains haven't created permanent and specific slots for incoming information. They sort the incoming sensory "mail" according to the shape and size of the envelope instead of the address. So they often put ideas together in new, unexpected, and creative ways.

That's why creative people are often young or seem so youthful and why extraordinary creative gifts are often demonstrated early in life. Albert Einstein developed his theory of relativity at the age of 23; Jesus confounded his elders in the temple when he was just 12; John Keats had written his great odes by the time he was 24; Mozart was a dazzling child prodigy; Joseph Smith received his first vision at the age of 14. To maintain a childlike freshness of perception, avoid narrow specialization. If you get too specialized, too narrow, your store of knowledge becomes obsolete and blocks present understanding and the stream of future learning.

Beware of the "left quadrant of the right nostril syndrome," trapping yourself through a narrow focus into a tiny corner of the canvas and never seeing the big picture. If you look at a face and all you see is a quadrant of nostril, you don't even see the nose, let alone the whole face. "'Tis not an eye or ear or nose we beauty call," said Alexander Pope, "but the joint force and full result of all."

To make something really new—to create anything substantial—you must see the big picture. Be curious about a lot of things. It isn't so much a matter of accumulating big piles of information. But have enough piles so that you can take something from this one, something from that one, and something from still another to combine and make uniquely new contributions. Scientists who come up with new ideas are continually crossing the boundaries of different domains. They go walking in many neighborhoods—across the street to physics, down the road to chemistry, then maybe take a stroll through biology.

My interest in a wide range of things—science, theology, sports, music, poetry—with their different rhythms and different dimensions, has helped me make connections and explore a world of new ideas. My interest is active—and I stay in motion. I still play squash a few times a week and write poems and songs to express, enlarge, and enhance my experience of life.

Completion

Completion is the hardest but most rewarding stage of the creative process. This is the stage at which you return to the rhythm of hard thinking and give final shape or direction to whatever you've been working on. This is more painful than conceiving the dream. To return to our birth cycle analogy, completion is the equivalent of having a baby. From what I've heard, that experience can be about as painful as anything you can imagine. Obert Tanner once said, "Creating a book is like having a baby. It's easier to conceive the idea than it is to deliver."

I don't mean to suggest that creative acts involve physical pain. But psychological pain can definitely be part of finishing a project. The pain of completion in the creative cycle has much to do with fear. There's a certain amount of security in keeping a project in the germination or assimilation stage. Completing something means offering it up for judgment. As long as you're just "workin' on it," you defer failure, but also the chance of true success. Ultimately, however, we are judged by what we finish, not what we start.

Completion is crucial for both the present project and future enterprises. Unless you complete your project—whether it's a special mission, business venture, a school report, a sonnet, or a song—it never attains the status of reality. It exists in a twilight zone of perpetual possibility. Imagine a farmer plowing a field and then never getting around to planting it because he thinks the furrows are a bit crooked. If you want to reap anything from life, you must finish your sowing.

Build Your Own Fire

The goal, as always, is to discover what works for you. Be your own person and make the most of your potential. Manage and protect the special fuel of life that has been entrusted to you and use it wisely while it burns. Learn the most efficient way to make your energy burn bright—not simply smolder.

Let's continue the analogy of building a fire to further illuminate the rhythm of the creative process. Building, tending, and keeping a fire going appeal to something primal in our DNA. Fire embodies the elements needed for survival—heat, light, and energy.

When you build a fire, you attend to the rhythm of the fire itself. You learn when to add fuel and when to let it breathe. You can't just toss on more wood, and you can't be forever stirring the embers. It's the same with the rhythm of creativity— you alternate activity and neglect, intense participation and letting well enough alone.

Building a fire requires kindling, structuring, and tending. You kindle a project by taking small, easily controlled steps. Without proper kindling to build energy, you won't get your creative fire going. But proceed beyond kindling, or your fire will die. You must add increasingly larger logs, leaving space for oxygen to enter.

People with little feel for the ongoing creative rhythm of life often neglect the structuring stage and toss a big log on a small fire. They haven't built up enough heat for the fire to grow. Pushing things too early will stunt the growth of any creative enterprise. You may get a flash, but no sustained glow. It's better to work wisely, pacing yourself with your own rhythms to avoid burnout.

Once your fire is burning, tend it by adding fuel and "letting it glow." The fire will burn while you're letting it alone. If you've entered into the prime rhythm of your creative activity, you won't need to poke at the fire, monitoring and manipulating your creative process. You will have learned to use your own precious fuel of life wisely while it burns.

8

TRUE GIVING

⌒∽o∽⌒

The central truth about the balance of life is "you reap what you sow." This is the Law of the Farm. Our ancestors lived on the land, working to the rhythm of planting and harvesting. If nothing was ventured, nothing was gained.

The rhythm of giving and getting is the divine generating force of life. You come into the world gasping to take in your first breath. You leave the world giving back your last breath. In the words of scripture, you "give up the ghost." During our life on earth, we continually take in air and give it back. The oxygen we breathe is a gift from living plants; our exhalation of carbon dioxide is our gift to plants.

We are always in the process of giving and receiving. The seeming paradox is that when you give, you automatically receive. You lose nothing by giving, which in fact enlarges you. Giving not only helps the recipient, but also enlarges and enhances the giver. The good teacher learns as much or more than the student. To truly receive, you must give without the expectation of return.

Human nature and the cycle of life are so constituted that receiving comes before giving. We seem to be biologically wired to be acquisitive; everyone is proud of certain acquisitions and accomplishments.

The process of acquiring generates the energy not only to survive but also to provide for others. The instinct to acquire keeps us alive and thriving; the danger is that it can become all-consuming. To quote once again the words of my mother, "Any virtue carried to an excess becomes a vice."

What happens in nature when the balance between getting and giving is upset? The Dead Sea takes in water, but because there's no outward flow, because it continually gets but doesn't give, its waters are stagnant, its shores sterile and uninviting. The same thing will happen to us if we only get and never give of our means. Though happiness cannot be bought, it is a byproduct of giving, caring, and serving.

The Drive to Acquire

When I was a kid growing up in Yuba City, California, times were hard, and it was tough to survive. I organized a small gang, mostly in self-defense. We used our fists and battled other kids in back alleys.

But the truth is that I didn't really ever feel tough inside. As a leader I wanted to be a nice guy. When my friends and I played cops and robbers, I always wanted to be the cop. When we dressed up like cowboys, I wanted to be the good guy wearing a white hat.

As I grew older, my instincts to protect and lead grew stronger. I wanted my "gang" to stay out of trouble, to act in positive and gainful ways. But I still wanted to win a fight when it came along. It was hard to relinquish the belief that I had to fight, and hard to abandon the conviction that I needed superior force and bravado to survive.

The instinct to fight to survive has stayed with me. That disposition is not necessarily negative, nor is it entirely selfish. It depends on how it is used. The drive to acquire comes from the instinct to survive and the need to provide for the ones we love. Behind the drive to acquire is the old predatory instinct. That instinct is vestigial in human beings, but it is certainly not extinct. In a real way, all of us are "predators," differing only in the means employed to achieve our ends. The predatory instinct can fuel uncontrolled aggressive behavior and asserts itself in war, where it can be frightening in its naked power.

In nature we see the predatory instinct in its pure form, predator and prey enacting the cycle of life and death, playing their parts in maintaining the balance of nature. Human civilization, however, demands the sublimation of raw predatory instinct, channeling it into individual assertion, ambition, and acquisition. You see the predatory instinct at work especially in ambitious people born into poverty. I think of my father, still a teenager when he had to get out there and be a provider in a rough-and-tumble world. He learned how to grub off the ground, using the tools at hand to master his particular environment and provide for his family.

When there is a winner and a loser, the balance wheel of society is thrown out of kilter. For there to be win/win outcomes, the predatory instinct must be transmuted into positive energy that is reciprocal and beneficial. Then we can acquire what we need without depriving others of what they need.

To this day, I still acquire things to benefit my family, friends, and employees—my "gang." But now we work together using the "muscle" between the ears rather than our fists.

As I was growing up, I believed the way to succeed was to acquire, prevail, and control. I wanted to master every situation and control my environment. Later on I did that quite literally by investing in land. There's nothing as enduring as real estate. You build from the ground up, and if you own the ground, you control the space and what's built on it. You take increasing stewardship of your environment.

In other areas, I took control of my intellectual environment by innovating components, then patenting total systems. For example, I invented the Intraflo device—which prevents blood clots at intravenous or intra-arterial sites—then marketed it as a total system. I'm doing the same thing today with Sorenson Vision. We're developing a system of products designed to make "real time interactive" video telephony of sound and sight available globally. Sorenson Vision's system includes our SVX chip, a phone, a computer or television, and a camera.

I have had the good fortune to be able to provide for my family, create work for hundreds of thousands of people, while improving the health and lives of millions. Wealth may bring a measure of security, but the responsibility it brings can breed caution and anxiety. You begin to lose your balance when your possessions begin to possess you.

Earlier in my life, accumulation was everything. The more I had, the more I wanted. Shadowed by insecurity and vague dissatisfaction, I remained convinced that I'd reach a point where enough would be enough, and I'd have so much that I'd arrive happy on the shores of complete contentment. So I continued the game of accumulation. I liked to keep score, but still the trophy of contentment eluded me. My compulsion was to top my latest achievement.

Then I reasoned that I could double my wealth and help twice as many people by simply doubling my efforts. But no matter how hard I worked and no matter how much I acquired, I found myself in a state of growing stress and discontent. I was constantly afraid of losing everything. The paradox of possession began to work against me. I discovered that the more you possess, the more your possessions possess you. And the more things you want—the more you become enslaved by them.

As my compulsion to accumulate things grew, I became trapped on a treadmill, and the faster I ran, the more I seemed to fall behind. I forgot the vital needs of my authentic self. Countless evenings I was persuaded to sit in meetings and on committees, somehow convinced they were more important than my own needs or the needs of my family. I left a sick son at home or a daughter who wanted help with homework, as I went off to some corporate or community function. My imbalance continued to grow.

I started to see every situation as the final opportunity, the ultimate chance, the last hope. I was like a desperate man in the desert. But the oasis I was running toward was a mirage.

I didn't see my way out of this trap until I was almost fifty years old. That's when it dawned on me that with the attitude of accumulation, no matter how much material wealth I gained, it would never be enough. The words of my wise mother began echoing through my mind: "Security is not in having wealth, it's knowing what things you can do without."

I began to realize that I needed to place more value on the things I could give than on the things I could get, that hanging on must be balanced with letting go. It was then that a sense of balance began coming back into my life, and I gradually came to know that an obsession with getting can be balanced only with the habit of giving. Attend to nature's ultimate rhythm, breathing in and breathing out. Taking in air at birth, letting it all out at death. This wisdom transcends Christianity. The nirvana of Buddhism is equivalent to Christ's "giving up the ghost," the ultimate letting go, the ultimate act of mortality.

Letting Go

In our everyday world, the quest to accumulate personal wealth must be balanced with the art of letting go. There's another paradox at work in the getting and giving of wealth: it's harder to give wealth away wisely than it is to acquire it. Philanthropy has its own laws of balance, wisdom, and love.

A few years ago I went through one of the most difficult periods of my life, when I tried to donate millions of dollars to the University of Utah Medical School. I had been approached to have the school named after me in exchange for a substantial gift. While working through that difficult situation, I learned a valuable lesson: We can get out of balance by focusing too much on making money, but we can also get out of balance by giving money away for the wrong reasons. When ego becomes part of the mix, the larger self tilts way out of balance and the joy of giving is lost. The experience with the medical school taught me that you only experience the joy of giving if you expect nothing in return.

The expectation of getting nothing in return is vital to the three-part process of setting the stage, shopping the options, and shedding the accumulated excess. The life of each of us should vibrate to this three-beat rhythm.

Giving and getting works in this rhythm, both in the material sphere of making a living and in the spiritual sphere of rearing a family. Being a parent has taught me the most about giving and getting. In our early years the emphasis is on the getting and the begetting; we set the stage by starting families and acquiring wealth. While you are getting all you can to provide for your children, you are also giving all you can to rear them. You give them life and your time, energy, and love.

At the fulcrum of getting and giving is shopping the options. This is the point at which you begin to "cash in" on your learning and hard work to reap rewards.

Shedding the excess completes the cycle of life, as you begin giving in a conscious and deliberate way. Shedding the excess helps you to see the profound exchange between getting and giving. I like the way Lillian Gish put it: "What you get is a living; what you give is a life."

The rhythm of parenting necessarily reflects the shedding process. I certainly don't want to imply that children are an "excess" to be shed, but they do grow up and leave, and their leaving teaches us a lesson about the rhythm of life. In a three-step process, we set the stage for them, we help them shop their options, and finally we let them embark upon their own separate lives. We must let go and let them go into the world.

It's like those training wheels on bicycles—we set our children on the bike, give them a shove, and watch as they wobble down the sidewalk. After they learn how to steer and keep their balance, we remove the training wheels and let them ride off. We shed our children only in the sense that we must ultimately give them total freedom.

The family becomes a microcosm of the larger world into which we're born. Everyone has a part to play and for the family to thrive there must be balance. My children, like all children, were born with different personality traits, drives, attitudes, and gifts. In my stewardship as a parent, I try very hard to help them equalize and balance their various gifts. Parents must strive to be fair and rejoice in their children's accomplishments—large and small.

A crucial factor in attaining family balance is what Robert Coles calls the "mutuality of moral guidance." Parents and children learn from each other. As parents instruct by example and precept, they exercise and strengthen their own moral sense. In the process, children develop their own conscience. Moral guidance has been weakened in our country by the proliferation of one-parent families. In recent years there's been a threefold increase of such families. This constitutes a devastating blow to children who, without both a mother and a father, end up shortchanged, often feeling lonely, abandoned, and even rejected.

The family should be a perfect example of balance in motion as children grow up and move out of the home. Ideally, they, too, become parents and participants in a new triad of father, mother, and child. Thus does the mutuality of moral guidance continue.

The Three Kinds of Giving

We all know the admonition that it's better to give than to receive. It's a truism uttered so often that its real meaning has become obscured. But behind the platitude is a profound truth.

First, let's look at the different ways of giving. There are three kinds: 1) You can give with the idea of getting something equal in return. This is giving as trading. 2) You can give with the expectation of eventually getting more. This is giving as investing. 3) You can give without any idea of getting anything in return. This is the true way of giving. And, as is usually the case, the third way is the best way.

When kids are told that it's better to give than to receive, they are understandably puzzled, for all they have known is getting. Consider the newborn, who is totally dependent, gasping for breath and then feeding at its mother's breast. Biology has wired human beings for survival by making infancy and early childhood a period of getting, getting, and more getting.

As my rabbi friend observed, we come into the world gasping, grasping, and grabbing. We come into this life as complete takers. Babies must constantly take or they will die. But as we grow up, the equation should begin to shift a little. The getting must give way to the giving as we participate in the continually changing whole of God's creation.

Try to convince a three-year-old to share a toy with a playmate, and you discover that learning to give is secondary to the drive to get all they can. They have been on the receiving end all of their lives and they like it that way. Kids like to hang onto things. Their instinct to acquire things is abetted by their parents, whose instinct is to take care of them and give them all they need for optimum survival.

Kids get gifts on their birthdays, gifts at Christmas, gifts when Mom and Dad return from trips. They grow up not questioning that things will be provided for them. They expect the world to give them things. Many adults still act the same way. It is so easy to forget the giver. In our giving and getting we forget that the ultimate giver of all is God.

Even though we learn to share and give as we grow older, we still have feelings and wants that haven't progressed all that much from the cradle. We are fearful that no one will like us, no one will feed us, no one will shelter us, no one will love us. We hang onto our adult "toys"—our material possessions—hugging them as a hedge against loneliness, insecurity, and destitution.

Giving As Trading

Making the transition to the most rudimentary reciprocity is hard. Even the first kind of giving—giving as trading—can at first be tough for kids. All they've known is getting. Why should they ever give something in return? It takes mature thought to comprehend the concept of reciprocity. The only way kids learn the first way of giving is to get something immediately in return. This is the instinct of "tit for tat." But they want something concrete in return, and they want it in exchange. They do not immediately comprehend the abstract idea of giving something now and getting something later. Delayed getting is still a species of the first kind of giving, but it's a necessary step toward an appreciation of the second kind of giving, which is giving to get more. Delayed getting and giving involves a disparity between the original act and the eventual reaction. It involves a longer rhythm and a longer attention span.

Christmas and birthday parties teach us how to cope with the delayed gratification of getting after we've given. At Christmas, the "trading" is pretty quick, but everyone knows how eager we are to open our own gifts. Children especially are much more interested in their own gifts than the ones they give. It's amusing how the young grandkids will quickly compare the gifts they get. We see kids grabbing their brother's action figure or their sister's Beanie Baby. The grass is always greener—or the toy is always better—if it belongs to someone else!

Birthday parties socialize kids into delayed gratification. At Christmas, you might have to wait a minute or two to receive, after you've given. Kids' birthday parties stretch the giving/getting rhythm over several months. Kids seldom pay much attention to what they're taking to the party because Mom usually picks up the present for them. But at least the children are being initiated into a broadening giving/getting ritual. We incorporate these rituals of reciprocity to teach the ideal that it's better to give than to receive. The expectation of return continues into adulthood; it is difficult learning how to give with a pure and unselfish heart.

Giving As Investing

The second kind of giving—giving as investing—promises a return of more than you have given. Like the first kind of giving, the second appeals to our selfish instincts. In fact, giving as investing is even more selfish and can become greed of the worst kind. This kind of giving can lead to usury, which is lending or trading money at an exhorbitant rate of return. The interest on the money can soon grow to more than the original amount lent. Our democratic society has wisely instituted laws against this kind of financial piracy, but there are those who still practice usury in different ways to take advantage of the poor and the desperate.

This second kind of giving does have a positive dimension, and it is this I want to emphasize. To really work, the giving must be unselfish and disinterested. This is the true and wise investment at the heart of true fellowship. This kind of giving is the heart of charity and rewards the giver in innumerable and unforeseen ways.

Unfortunately, the word *charity* today carries an official, do-your-duty kind of tone. For many, charity is not prompted by the Christian sense of active love. Instead, it's embodied in a big container in a parking lot where you toss things you no longer need or want so you can take a tax deduction. The idea that charitable giving involves making some kind of huge sacrifice is contrary to the true rhythm of giving and getting. One of my favorite sayings is, "Don't give until it hurts. Give until it feels good."

Kindness is a hard thing to give away—it keeps coming back. A little love goes a long way. And a lot of love goes forever. So love life, and it will give back to you in countless ways that cannot be measured. A thousand people can love us without changing us a particle. It's our loving them that changes us for the better.

No one has ever become poor by giving. But all that you are unable to give possesses you. Learn how to shed the excess. Just as energy is never lost as it is converted into different forms, whatever excess we shed, whatever we give away, is never truly lost. The greatest benefit of a gift is the love that's generated with the giving. We shouldn't be discouraged if our giving isn't always understood or acknowledged; kind giving has its influence still. The heart that gives, gathers.

An old painting called "The Gatherers" shows women gathering the harvest, each holding sheaves close to her bosom, an illustration that we reap what we sow. Giving is equivalent to sowing. What you reap from giving is a new life. In a real sense, the heart that gives grows through its gathering.

Pure Giving

The two kinds of giving we've been exploring—giving as trading and giving as investing—can be ennobled by purity of motive. Each kind of giving is justified by an appeal to self-interest. "You want to get something? Well, you have to give something." We've all heard this as in "If you want to get a letter, you've got to send a letter." Today the equation is, "You must send e-mail to receive e-mail." Practically, it makes a lot of sense. Many actions that promote the common good have their origin in self-interest. If giving increases the common store of knowledge and happiness, the motive behind the giving isn't relevant.

Motive, however, is at the heart of spiritual growth and True Balance. Here we enter the third dimension of pure giving. Pure giving knows no season. We give with no notion of getting anything in return. "Blessed are those who can give without remembering." Don't be forever keeping score, shouting your gracious acts. The more you forget about your good deeds, the more you will be remembered for them.

Pure giving includes material gifts and follows the injunction of Jesus to give to the poor. Pure giving is really giving of yourself. By spending yourself, you become rich—not in gold, but rich in love and spirit. It's a way of encountering the world, grateful we've received so much more from the Creator than we can ever give. The richest man on earth is but a pauper fed and clothed by the bounty of heaven. The best way to attract fortunate events into your life is to surprise others with unexpected gifts. Your gifts to others give you True Balance.

Pure giving is the proper response to the idea that to whom much has been given, much is required. The more you possess, the greater the responsibility to share. In sharing we contribute to the great balance of nature and attain balance in ourselves.

To Love Is to Give

Pure giving is prompted by love. It's possible to give without loving, but it's impossible to love without giving. Giving is more a dictate of the heart than a command of the brain. Therefore, cultivate an educated and a grateful heart, schooled in unselfishness.

The educated heart sets the balance between giving and receiving. Just as one learns to give, one must learn to receive. Only by giving can you enlarge your soul to receive unselfishly. Unless you can give with "no strings attached," with no thought of return, you won't be able to truly receive the gifts of others. There is a rhythm between the two that is achieved when you realize that the two are one. Giving is receiving—receiving is giving; that is the secret to the true joy of living.

I want to conclude this section with three thoughts that sum up what I've been writing about. The first is from Albert Einstein: "The value of a man should be in what he gives and not in what he is able to receive."

The second comes from someone in a field far from Einstein's theoretical physics. Danny Thomas said this about the rhythm of getting and giving: "Success has nothing to do with what you personally gain in life or accomplish for yourself. It's all in what you do for others."

Finally,

> It is in *loving,* not in *being loved,*
> That the heart finds its quest;
> It is in *giving,* not in *getting,*
> That our lives are truly blest.

9

BALANCE OF
SELF AND OTHERS

∽ᴏ∾

We are social creatures. It is in the shelter of each other that we live and prosper. One human being alone is an incomplete human being. We need others and they need us. Only by working together can we devise tools, build machines, and transform the environment. I am reminded that the Greek word for *idiot* originally meant someone who lived alone. It was assumed that anyone cut off from other people would go crazy. The ancient Greeks, steeped in the idea of the Golden Mean, knew that interaction with fellow human beings was necessary to keep one's self in balance.

We need other people to grow. You never see a giant redwood tree standing alone. Its shallow root structure makes it vulnerable to the wind. Standing together, redwood trees have tremendous strength because their roots intertwine to hold each other up. It's the same with people. Human beings are incorrigibly social creatures. We warm each other with our love.

We're somewhat like porcupines in a storm, who need to be close enough to stay warm, but not so close that we poke each other. We need a balance of solitude and fellowship, just as we need the rhythm of rest and activity. We need to get away by ourselves—to ponder and meditate the progress of our lives, to reevaluate our choices, and to reaffirm our goals.

But we shouldn't get so far away that we turn ourselves into pitiful characters like Howard Hughes. He once had everything, but in the end had nothing. I think a living hell might be the loneliness of having everything and deciding that it isn't enough. Having everything, Hughes ended up a lonely old man, surrounded by hired servants and favor-seekers, wondering why so few people loved him. He became a one-dimensional, pathetic person, possessed of fabulous wealth but stripped of the relationships that would have truly enriched his life.

With their entourage of lackeys, servants, and sycophants leading them into eccentric excess, wealthy people are always in danger of getting out of balance. With that in mind, I work hard to keep my life balanced. I keep my office modest and spartan, which helps keep me in touch with what matters most.

A basic part of maintaining balance for me is seeking periods of solitude and meditation. Solitude and meditation help me "stand outside" myself, so I can see myself as part of the whole. I try to see where I've been, where I am, and where I want to go.

To catch a glimpse of a "bigger picture," I used to go up on Salt Lake's east bench and look down at the city to get a sense of where it was moving. I'd ask myself, "What's the traffic flow? How fast are the neighborhoods growing and where are they likely to grow?" Then I'd buy land in the line of development and bet on the future.

Find the promising "east benches" of your life where you can see where you've been, where you are, and where you want to go. If you don't, you may find yourself being pushed, elbowed, and jostled by your fellow porcupines. Be the master of your environment. Put the flow of life and the moving world to work for you, too. Gain and develop perspective by separating yourself from the crowd and seeing the three-dimensional nature of all things.

Know Who You Are

To become a truly balanced individual, everyone needs to separate in some degree from siblings, from parents, from neighborhood, and from community. Jesus taught this when he said that a man must leave his mother, and a woman must leave her home. Some degree of separateness is necessary to be a person in your own right. If you don't have a balanced sense of yourself, you will be susceptible to various pressures from family, peers, or colleagues. Emerge from your childhood view of the world in which circumstances and environment have been the controlling forces in your life. Become independent. Don't just react to circumstances—act to create your own. Think for yourself and control your environment by *learning, knowing,* and *understanding* who you are and where you want to be.

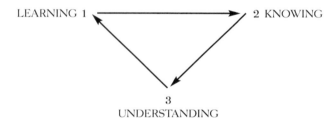

Figure 26– The Learning Process

When you are a fully emancipated, independent, and confident person, who wisely exercises agency and assumes responsibility, your love for family, friends, and community grows. By understanding where you begin and others leave off, you take control of the interrelated rhythm of God, self, and others.

When you develop the right balance of *God, self,* and *others,* you not only relate more successfully with friends, but you also better understand enemies. Jesus said to love your enemies.

Sometimes we have to love those who are the hardest to toler-
ate because they contribute more to our growth than those who
make things easy for us. Some people are harder to love, but
they are often the ones who need our love and understanding
the most.

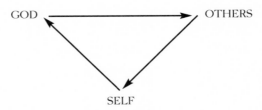

Figure 27– Triad of Oneself

You've heard the cliché that opposites attract. Like many
clichés, it has a significant element of truth. And that truth has
to do with balance. If two people are too much alike, chances
are in time they won't be able to stand each other. When there
is enough difference, whether in temperament, personality, or
interests, the relationship can develop that necessary third
dimension within which each of us can achieve balance.

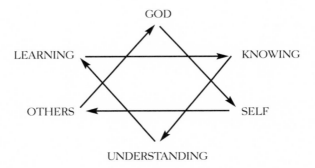

Figure 28– Interposed Triads Illustrating Identity and Life Processes

Walt Whitman, the poet who more than any other cele-
brated individual freedom and social attachment, said: "Have
you learned lessons only from those who admire you and who
are tender with you and stand beside you? Have you not
learned great lessons from those who braced themselves against
you and disputed with you in the journey of life?"

As Whitman recognized, we need the spur of conflict, competition, and, yes, sometimes even defeat. From these come
true strength, character, and spiritual growth. From adversity,
we learn the skills of survival.

We, like trees, survive not by resisting, but by submitting to
the wind, then springing up straighter and stronger after the
storm.

Eternal Benefit

The happiest people I know are those who care more about
others than they do about themselves. Help others to like
themselves a little better and rest assured they will like you very
much. When we seek to discover the best in others, we naturally bring out the best in ourselves. As sure as day follows
night, those who bring sunshine into the lives of others will
light up their own lives. The best way to feel good about yourself is to do something to make someone else's life better. When
we do this and reach out to help others, we find that greater
love flows back to us.

Let us love people by our actions. A little individual kindness bestowed on an individual does more good than having a
vast but impersonal love for all humankind. Love one human
being purely, warmly, and honestly, and you will be loved.
When you are in the service of your fellowmen, life is full of
meaning. Love is the only service that power and money can't
command. What you do for yourself is fleeting and dies with
you. What you do for others continues and flows eternally. The

poorest father sometimes leaves his children the richest inheritance—his love.

Balance of Self and God

We maintain balance by seeing God as the third dimension in all things. Once we discover God, we balance with our Creator and joy abounds. With God, all things are possible.

We balance our lives three dimensionally just as God has so delicately, precisely, and tenderly balanced and nurtured our world. God's creative balancing in all of nature is the secret of life. He has constructed the human soul in such a way that only goodness brings about True Balance. Living in harmony with God encourages us to make choices that enrich our lives. The more space we give to God in our lives, the more at home we feel within ourselves. We find true reality and balance in our lives when our faith calls forth God's helping hand.

Look at the larger sphere of life all about us. We are immersed in a most beautiful environment. God pulls upward the trees, grasses, and all living things. All this is done against the force of gravity in a three-dimensional balancing act while in motion.

This is not only true of nature, but of ourselves as well. God pulls us upward and outward, glorifying us. Even as the sun makes the plants and trees grow taller, our great Creator calls upon us to grow tall in spirit, to become more than we are. Our power is in the choice and agency of becoming. This idea was expressed when Christ asked, "What manner of men ought ye to be? Verily, I say unto you, even as I am" (3 Nephi 27:27). We are all at our best when we imitate him in our relationships with one another and in our dealings with ourselves. Then we move into balance, our smaller wheel spiraling upward and outward within the balanced orb of God's creation.

A Lost Dimension

So often in our lives, God is the lost third dimension, or at best a fictional dimension. But belief and faith in God is essential for us to experience fullness of life. You may try to build a life without God and manage to do it to some extent, but a fundamental dimension will always be missing. Wholeness of being and joy are found in knowing God. Life without God is like living in a dim corner of a shack rather than in the brilliant expanse of his holy temple. Within each of us is the presence of God in all its fullness, majesty, and glory. When we realize we are truly made in the image and likeness of God, when we feel and know the divine possibilities within us, we experience the divine "I am." "Know ye not that ye are the temple of God, and that the spirit of God dwelleth in you?" (1 Corinthians 3:16).

The secular belief is that we alone determine our own destiny. But such a notion signals a certain arrogance. It denies the other two dimensions—God and others. It is possible to feel so self-sufficient that you become a law unto yourself. Worst of all you lose the sense of gratitude. The greatest of all virtues is gratitude, and lack of gratitude is our greatest barrier to intellectual and spiritual growth. Gratitude unexpressed is ingratitude.

Some people move beyond themselves and make the second dimension of self and others the whole of their being. This is superior to egocentric self-pride, but unless God is present as a third dimension, relationships with others will ultimately fall short. Relationships with others, no matter how profound and no matter how intimate, can never approximate our relationship with God. With God as the ground of our being, as the necessary third dimension, relationships with others take on a transforming depth and richness. Instead of fumbling in the dark, we are infused with hope, faith, and light. We are blessed with his love.

Plant the Seed

Belief in God begins by taking a hypothetical, scientific, experimental approach. Accept God, his word and theory, pray fervently, and live a life in accordance with his teachings. Following the word of God might be compared to planting a seed. As you try this experiment you will begin to feel better about yourself, other people, and life as a whole. Care for the seeds you've planted. Even a good seed dies if it isn't nurtured. As you live according to God's will, you will experience the love he has for every single human being.

For me, the fact that God exists is not an issue. I don't doubt that there is a Creator. Intuition, emotion, and prayer tell me that God, a creator, exists. I have progressed beyond that basic question. I trust and love my Father in heaven, and I know he loves me and each and every one of his creations.

Believe It, Test It, Do It

The beauty of putting trust in God is that he is always there. But we must call upon his presence. Choosing to trust God is an act of will and faith. Remember the Sermon on the Mount, "Seek, and ye shall find; knock, and it shall be opened unto you" (Matt. 7:7). First knock. Once you accept God's word, you'll receive his knowledge and gain the understanding and wisdom to become as he is.

To understand God's will, study the scriptures, heed the prophets, and pray from the heart. Apply three more principles: believe it, test it, and do it. This is the process we all must go through. If it feels right, sounds right, and works right, we know we are on the right track. Christ taught, "If any man will do his will, he shall know of the doctrine, whether it be of God, or whether I speak of myself" (John 7:17).

Ye Are Gods

A turning point in my life was coming to recognize that every human being is a son or daughter of God, who can some-day become as God is. Our potential is the oak asleep in the acorn. When that truth burst upon my consciousness, it fueled me with a passion to excel.

I am moved by Christ's response when he was about to be stoned for claiming to be the Son of God. He says to his tor-mentors, quoting from their own scriptures, "Is it not written in your law, . . . Ye are gods?" (John 10:34). The discovery that I am of God's species made me realize what eternity offers. It increased my love of God and my desire to keep his commandments.

Knowing that you can become as God is extremely hum-bling. This might seem a contradiction. But knowing that you can become as God makes you realize your human limitations. It keeps you from acting as though you are already a god, as so many do when they deny the existence of the Lord. You become acutely conscious that you have a long, long way to go.

Do the right thing, and follow God's example. He does not operate for his own pleasure; he is concerned about the poor, the broken hearted, the outcast. Nor does he work alone, but with his Son, Jesus Christ, and the Holy Ghost, as part of an eternal triad. He invites all of us to be his disciples, participat-ing in his work, which he has defined for us: "This is my work and my glory—to bring to pass the immortality and eternal life of man" (Moses 1:39).

Co-Creators with God

Not only are men and women created in God's image and in embryo like him, but he has vested in us the power to become co-creators with him by bringing about new life. This sacred privilege of parenthood is the source of some of the greatest joy in life as well as life's most significant challenges.

Anyone engaged in creative work is, in the humblest of ways, a co-creator with God. As a simple and obvious example, someone "discovers" something new, claims it as his knowledge, patents it, and becomes an inventor. Actually, in the smallest, humblest, limited way, an inventor imitates how God organized matter, balanced it, and molded the creation of all things.

We can forget that God is the source of our creative power. We attribute our creative instincts to innate physical gifts, which are actually nothing more than gifts from God. As a result, we fail to recognize the source of our own creative spiritual dimension.

The Power of Prayer

All too often, we just pay lip service to our spiritual dimension. Developing our spiritual side must include more than attending church and piously intoning a litany of belief. It is not enough to just go through the motions. In fact, when the spiritual dimension is truly activated, going through the motions is irrelevant. A good example of this is prayer. We don't have to isolate ourselves or pray at specifically appointed times. We can pray wherever we are, no matter what we're doing, whenever we need strength or feel the need to ask for help or give thanks. Prayer is a spiritual disposition, not a physical posture.

Prayer is something we can always call upon. A song I wrote called "I Do Believe" has a verse I've often silently repeated:

> He who knows my every need,
> Help me while I try to lead;
> Lead me, help me see so high.

Because you pray from your heart and your heart is always with you, the strength available through prayer is instantly accessible. But prayer must be followed up by action and repentance. Some people would rather pray for forgiveness than fight temptation.

Early in life, I realized how I chose to behave was the product of my attitude in any given circumstance. Attitude is all-important; it determines your reality. A humble, grateful attitude grows out of love and enhances your life many times over. In the process of loving, a change accrues internally and radiates love and light to your environment, and you share in God's victories. You take a step closer to him, and once again, in a great act of faith and love, you right your own balance.

Example, Example, Example

Once you understand that you are a son or daughter of God, you realize the responsibility you bear toward your own sons and daughters. You are a role model whether you want to be or not. I know that my grandchildren and great-grandchildren are watching me like little angels with eagle eyes.

We influence our posterity by our example, showing and teaching them God's truths. Children already feel and know the truth intuitively, much more than we know. But mostly they need to see truth in action; they need and want to see it in you. As Albert Schweitzer taught, "There are only three ways of raising children: example, example, and example."

They need to know that you care about them. I'm thankful also that when my children go to church, they'll be taught the same principles I'm trying to impart. But they need to go beyond merely attending a church. They must internalize these principles and make them the basis of their everyday thinking and doing.

By internalizing these principles, children develop the capacity to act freely, balancing their lives in their own way. Loving parents impart their principles and send their children into the world as special, unique, and independent individuals.

In this regard, I want to update and include a little essay I wrote in 1964.

The Game of Life

I am giving you the ball, my child, and making you quarter-back on our team. Because in this game of life, the Great Referee will soon select a time to call me out.

Through your life thus far, I have been your father, your guardian, and your coach. So I'll hand it to you straight . . . there is only one game on our schedule of life, and that is the "Big Game." The Big Game is going to last your whole life. At times it will seem very long and tiring because there are no time outs and no substitutes. You must play every down, without relief, and you have to stay in there until the final whistle blows.

Your heredity, training, and environment have given you a great backfield to help you, and they have won a wide reputation for dependability; their names are Faith, Hope, and Charity. You are also fortunate that you will be working behind a sturdy line; end-to-end, they are: Loyalty, Devotion, Enthusiasm, Respect, Study, Cleanliness, and Honesty.

As your father and coach, I would advise you to stay focused on the goal posts, which by some have been called the "Pearly Gates." Your Creator is the referee and sole official. He makes the rules, and there is no appeal.

There are ten basic rules; you know them as the Ten Commandments. You are the quarterback, so you must abide by them strictly, according to the dictates of your own heart and conscience.

There is also an important ground rule. It is: "As ye would that men should do to you, do ye even so to them." In this big game of life, if you lose the ball, you lose the game, because you cannot score without the ball.

Now this is the ball—It is your immortal soul. Hold onto it, and go in there and play your heart out!

So long, my child. I'll be seeing you later.

All my eternal love, Dad

EPILOGUE:
CONTINUITY

❦

Life does not conclude but continues eternally.

To continue means to go forward, to strive, to endure. Continuity conveys the idea of moving forward while maintaining links to what has gone before. This continuity is the essence of True Balance.

Staying in motion is basic to True Balance. Too often balance is seen as mere equilibrium. It is thought by many to connote something static, quiescent, at rest; but True Balance is ever changing, dynamic, and charged with vital energy.

We can see the principles of True Balance at work in the concept of continuity. The three crucial aspects of continuity are extension, persistence, and duration. Just as True Balance is comprised of dimension, motion, and rhythm, so is continuity:

Extension corresponds to dimension.
Persistence corresponds to motion.
Duration corresponds to rhythm.

The continuity of True Balance is like an ascending helix. From above, the helix looks two-dimensional, a circle inscribed over and over again. But observed from the side, the helix is seen to be ascending through three dimensions, moving ever upward. It's going over the same territory but at an increasingly higher plane. So what appears to be closure is actually continuity.

To expand the analogy, think of a spiral, which also ascends in a circular manner, but expands outward at the same time. Now we have true three-dimensional motion, with the rhythm of the continual orbit of the ever-expanding and ever-ascending circle.

Continuity prospers only with True Balance and is evidenced throughout the universe in things both great and small. Subatomic electrons and protons are engaged in a continual rhythmic dance—drawing near, then pushing away. The rhythm of the expanding and contracting universe is recapitulated even in the throbbing of the human heart.

Poets of old rhapsodized about the music of the spheres, where the planets and stars moved in rhythmic harmony. So too we as individuals must find harmony among the spheres within which we move. We are at our best when we continually balance our physical, intellectual, and spiritual dimensions.

We are most human when we strive to imitate God and his creative force. God is the true Third Dimension and without his presence, our personal world would be only a two-dimensional, flat circle. Acknowledging God's creative force transforms the flat circle of inert matter into the burgeoning globe of teeming life. The three-dimensional nature of all things proves his wondrous existence.

The creative principle is most simply and profoundly expressed as "God created the world." We imitate God by creating what we love, and loving what we create. Loving and creating come together in true giving, which is the most godlike triad of human living.

True giving is most profoundly demonstrated in bringing children into the world. We love our children without reservation, condition, or expectation. The irreducible trinity of man, woman, and child is the most sacred manifestation of truth, balance, and continuity. Two come together as one to produce a third, and a new generation grows up as the older generation lovingly, slowly, and inexorably "gives way." The passing of one generation and the springing up of a new generation tells us that life does not conclude but rather continues. What seems like closure is really recycling and continuity.

In True Balance, closure is always continuity, a conclusion is always an introduction, and an ending is always a beginning.

I am awed continually by the example and life of Christ, and as I make my own journey through life, I consciously want to live fully, completely, and bravely and feel as Christ did, saying, "Father, not as I will, but as thou wilt." His is *the* glorious example of the ultimate, complete, abundant, giving-back of a perfect, balanced life.

> The adventure of life is to learn.
> The purpose of life is to grow.
> The nature of life is to change.
> The challenge of life is to overcome.
> The essence of life is to care.
> The opportunity of life is to serve.
> The secret of life is to dare.
> The spice of life is to befriend.
> The beauty of life is to give.